The Scent of Lavender

The Scent of Lavender

Finding Peace in Letting Go

Kim Corder

ISBN: 979-8-9930385-0-6

K.C. Incorporated HSP

2487 S Gilbert Rd, Gilbert, AZ 85295

Contents

Chapter 1
My Story

I always believed in my heart that my beloved yet departed grandmother would one day visit me in my dreams. She was, after all, more like a mother to me than my own. Our connection and conversations weren't just deep, they were soul level. She was my mentor in life and my muse in all things creative.

It had been years since her passing—with zero celestial communication, no dream-visits, no muse-like channeling from another realm...nothing. Eventually my memories of her began to fade into the background of my busy, adult life. All expectations that our soul connection would continue, even if only through REM sleep, had long been put to rest.

Years later, she did finally visit me in my dreams. At first, this dream seemed meaningless. Sometime later, it made so much sense and actually became a pivotal moment in my life that changed everything.

I should have known she would make a memorable entrance in an unforgettable way—she always did. I should have expected the topic of her visit to be a weighty one. In true form, she wanted to discuss an issue in my life that I had been trying to ignore for quite some time. She always had a way of making the heavy things seem lighter...more manageable.

My subconscious knew there was a pressing issue that needed to be dealt with, yet I reasoned it best that it be swept under a rug and ignored, at least for a while. After all, I was busy raising our 4 children. Being constantly pulled in so many directions just didn't allow me the bandwidth or ability to deal with any life-altering issues just then.

Yet here sat my grandmother, next to me on the same old familiar bench I grew up sitting on with her. This was where we always had our heart conversations.

"I know this is hard honey, but today is the day that we clean out this room," she said in a firm yet gentle way.

That metaphorical room my grandmother referred to is what I like to lovingly call 'my junk room' (think junk drawer on steroids). Only this room was filled with the kind of junk you can't just sort through and place in three piles: keep, donate, and throw away.

The only way to really 'clean out' this room was to examine and deal with all the hurts...and there were many. From childhood junk to the mess that was my marriage. There were bins of rejection, discouragement, and disappointment. Buckets of bitterness and unexplained hurtful memories...loads and loads of yuck and junk.

I decided that there was no way I was going to open that Pandora's box...not today and ideally (in my unhealthy mind) not ever! *! I'll* *just keep shoving the hurts into that room so I don't have to look at them.*

I snapped back—"No Grandma, I can't. The kids have piano lessons and soccer practice today, and I'm volunteering tonight. I know that room is a mess, but I just don't have the time to deal with it right now."

"Sweetheart, I know this is going to be hard for you, and I know this is not the best time to deal with all this mess. But, honey, today is THE DAY this room gets cleared out."

I awoke from the dream feeling frustrated and a bit annoyed. Why would my grandmother come to me this way? And why didn't she care that my life at the time was too busy to deal with that junk? How could she just keep repeating, "Today is the day this room will get cleaned out?"

The morning rushed in with the busyness of parenting young children, and it didn't take long for that unsettling dream to take a back seat to juggling schedules, taxiing kiddos, and the crazy life of a stay-at-home mother of four.

Still, there were undeniable supernatural forces at work that day. By the end of it, my grandmother's visit and words all made sense as the hidden messiness of my life came bursting out—against my will.

As I sat staring at the undeniable proof, I experienced the intense, heart-crushing pain of discovering my husband's many years of indiscretions.

With the same fervor that I started my day of child rearing, I ended my day, overwhelmed by betrayal. There were no words, only gasps and tears and pain.

There is a distinct physical pain that accompanies a broken heart. I sat, crumpled in a puddle of tears, repeating the words, "I have to stay strong for the kids." My mind needed to somehow make sense of it. This unique pain brands the heart with the searing burn of betrayal.

At first, I began to reach out to those closest to me, searching for comfort and compassion for my wounds. Sadly, many just didn't know what to say or how to help. Often, our society is uncomfortable around emotional or relational wounds, and there was an overwhelming sense that it was my job to 'hurry up and heal' so that I didn't make those around me uncomfortable.

I sought out spiritual counsel. Unfortunately, what they offered wasn't what I needed just then either. I needed empathy, yet what I received was others who personalized my situation and in that, couldn't help but to offer a whole lot of unsolicited advice.

Oh, to hear compassionate words like, "I don't know what I would do if I were in your shoes", or "I can't imagine how hard this must be for you". Or even "I'm so sorry for what you are going through", anything remotely resembling empathy would have been so soothing to my wounded soul.

In many ways, emotional wounds must be cared for in the same way as physical wounds. If ignored or mishandled, any wound will become infected. The same is true of a heart wound, only it becomes infected with things such as disappointment, the inability to trust, discouragement, unforgiveness, and worst of all... bitterness.

Maybe your concern isn't a recent wound—in fact, you have been carrying the weight of unforgiveness for so many years that at this point it doesn't feel like much of a weight at all. You have gotten used to carrying it.

Yet unforgiveness and bitterness are something that MUST be dealt with. Over time, undealt-with hurt builds up and begins to leak out into other areas of our lives.

It takes its toll: emotionally, relationally, physically, spiritually.

Unforgiveness will not, does not, and cannot lay dormant forever. One thing I know for sure is that if we do not deal with our unforgiveness, it will eventually deal with us.

Long-term wounds that have not been properly cared for have some serious side effects. One being...scar tissue.

Scar tissue is unique because its initial purpose is to protect us from further injury. When we harbor things such as disappointment, resentment, unforgiveness, or bitterness, it causes our heart to build up scar tissue. Initially for a good reason—to protect us from further injury. Yet in order to forgive and heal, we must expose the very thing that now has layers upon layers of scar tissue around it...our heart.

You see, forgiveness requires trust, and trust requires an open heart. In order to expose our heart, we must break down the scar tissue that has built up over the years. Exposing that original wound is necessary as it allows us to heal from the inside out. Sometimes the process of scar removal around our hearts can be excruciating.

Allow me to share a personal story about scar tissue.

My oldest daughter was born with a defect in her inner ear. Her eardrums were tilted, causing fluid to collect in them. She suffered countless ear infections in the first few years of her life, and eventually her hearing became dramatically impaired. We were referred to a specialist who took one look at her tiny ears and said she needed tubes put in right away to allow for drainage.

The doctors assured me this procedure would cure my little girl of her ear pain as well as improve her hearing loss, which in turn would help correct her speech impediment.

Over the next several years five sets of tubes were surgically placed in my daughter's tiny, stubborn eardrums. Each time, the process became more difficult because the surgeon had to cut through more scar tissue. The scar tissue had built up and was pushing those tubes out of her ears.

At one point the doctor became more concerned about the buildup of scar tissue than the original issue. There was talk of permanent hearing loss due to scar tissue.

I share this story to make a key point. Scar tissue is stubborn. It builds up over time and if left undealt with it will do more damage to a broken heart than the original wound. Emotional and relational scar tissue becomes a protective wall around the very thing we need to expose in order to heal—our sensitive heart.

While scar tissue may appear to protect us from further injury, it cannot and does not offer any healing in and of itself. It must be dealt with so that we can truly heal.

We all try to heal when wounded. With heart wounds, we may see a counselor or confide in a friend or family member. Or we seek out spiritual guidance, looking for words of wisdom or direction. We read all kinds of books on healing, and it seems to help for a while but eventually becomes too painful or too hard to continue the work. So we give up.

My Story

Stirring up unpleasant memories and working on our hurts is never easy or fun. No one gets excited about it. That would just be weird!

Many of us just stop trying because it gets too hard. The thought of trudging through all that past junk seems excruciating.

Unfortunately, each time we try and fail, we're gifted with another layer of stubborn scar tissue around our heart. This was my personal experience. I had attempted to let go and forgive for many years, with little or no success.

I needed more. Trying to force myself to forgive and move on was just not working. That is when I started looking at this process of forgiveness and acceptance in a different way. Instead of willing myself to change, I started focusing on the consequences or ramifications that I would experience if I never changed. What would happen if I never forgave or accepted what was done to me?

This became a defining moment for me because it allowed me to understand the why behind the need to forgive. It revealed that I did indeed need to forgive and let go of my hurts. NOT because the person who hurt me deserved forgiveness and certainly NOT because what was done to me was okay—it wasn't!

I needed to figure out how to forgive for one simple reason—so I could heal. The moment I understood that I started to sense a change in my heart.

One of the first things I did was look deeply at the damage that a scar-tissued heart does. Some of the consequences of a scar tissue layered heart:

Makes us more guarded so we don't allow others in. Scar tissue affects our ability to trust others.

Makes us unable to trust. That can build to a point where we question everyone's intentions.

Makes us more and more unhappy—possibly to the point where we are unable to find any true joy in life.

Makes us fly off the handle at the smallest offense. Our bucket of hurt is so full that even the smallest pebble of wrongdoing can send us over the edge.

We try dozens of times to get past the hurt, but nothing really helps so eventually we just stop trying. We push people away because something in your DNA believes they will eventually hurt us.

No doubt I've only touched the surface on the consequences of holding onto unforgiveness and bitterness. We will all undoubtedly experience personal consequences from holding onto hurts for too long. If you have some deeply rooted hurts, the thought of ever letting go of them may seem impossible to you. Trust me, I've been there, and I know exactly how you are feeling.

What I also know is that eventually all of us will come to a crossroads, and we must choose which path to take. The first choice is a path that leads us towards living a life of someone who might be characterized by one or more of the following:

bitterness, anger, judgment, unhappiness, in turmoil, lacking purpose, unable to find joy, sad, depressed, gloomy, critical, negative, on edge, harsh, nit-picky, unsympathetic, fault-finding, cruel, insensitive, abusive, rude, miserable...

Now let's look at the second path presented to us on that crossroad —choosing to live in denial.

This path is certainly an attractive one. Many of us will reason that if we can't get past the hurts, then we will just ignore them. Sounds like a rational choice to me.

There are three definitions of denial that I want to share with you:

1. Refusal to acknowledge the existence of something; refusing to believe or admit that something exists.
2. A state of mind marked by a refusal or an inability to recognize and deal with a serious personal problem.
3. A statement saying that something is not true or not correct.

Do any of these definitions describe you? We put a Band-Aid on it and tell ourselves, "It's not so bad. I'll be fine!" While this may feel better for a bit, the truth is, things are not 'just fine'!

I don't have to tell you that both of those path choices are detrimental to our health. Living in anger, bitterness, and unforgiveness, is damaging for obvious reasons. But did you know that denial also does a significant amount of damage?

First, denial hinders our emotions. Second, it keeps us from close relationships and third, it extends our pain. Denial can also be a catalyst for many other unhealthy behaviors. It can encourage us to:

- Lie (when we deny the facts)
- Be irresponsible (when we avoid responsibility by blaming, justifying or minimizing)
- Be unsympathetic (when we deny that our actions were as hurtful as they actually were) Be ignorant (when we deny that we are indeed in denial)

Trust me when I say that I'm just exposing the tip of the iceberg regarding the damage that denial does in our lives. It may feel like a quick fix but over time it is a costly mistake.

When we refuse to let go of hurts, we have chosen to walk one of those two paths. We are either bitter or we are in denial. Both paths lead to destruction.

Like me, you may be a seasoned traveler of both those paths. Something I've learned (the hard way) is that neither is the right path. Neither leads to healing, health, forgiveness or peace.

In 2008 I traveled to Germany to visit extended family. While there, one of the things I wanted to experience was driving on the Autobahn. I anticipated the thrill of driving on a freeway with no speed limit, and I intended to get behind the wheel and drive as fast as humanly possible (in a small stick shift vehicle).

Please understand my objective here was not that I had a death wish or that I longed to be a race-car driver. That wasn't it at all. In fact, the one and only reason I was intent on driving as fast as humanly possible on the Autobahn was simply because—I was allowed to.

You see, I am a rule follower. So, if the rule says that I can drive as fast as I want, then by golly I am going to drive fast! And let me tell you, when I got behind the wheel of that little German car, all reasonable thought and desire for safety literally flew out the window as I pushed that pedal to the metal. The idea of no speed limits was dangerously exhilarating.

That is how I envision both the path of unforgiveness and denial. Speeding one hundred miles per hour down any freeway is never the smartest choice of action. Yet it seemed right to me because there was nothing that said I couldn't. I barreled ahead with no thought regarding the possible destruction that I could have caused had there been an accident.

Thankfully, there is another path...a third choice. It's a difficult one to find and sadly, few actually find it.

While the other two paths are wide and welcoming, they also lead to destruction. This third path is narrow and hard to find yet it actually leads to healing and health in the form of forgiveness, acceptance and ultimately, peace.

Often this road seems too scary a path to even try going down. As you look, you will see the overgrowth and treacherousness along the path due to lack of use. Few have ventured on this journey. Forgiveness is after all, the road less traveled.

It took me a long time to find this road that leads to healing and even longer to navigate through it. That's why I wrote this book—to help others.

Together I know we can do this! Take my hand and let me help you. Let's lock arms and before you know it we'll be skipping along like Dorothy in Oz, down the yellow brick road (well, maybe not quite that easy or cute but you get the idea).

If you are reading these words—it's time to really deal with your hurts (past or present) so that you can move on. It's what the universe wants for you...it's what's best for you!

Some of you, right now may be reading this and thinking, "No way, not going to happen. I can read this (another) book on forgiveness but I'm not sure I can truly forgive the hurt that has been done. It doesn't seem possible!"

Well, all I have to say to that is...EXCELLENT! PERFECT! That is exactly where you need to be in order to start this journey.

Why, you ask? Let's find out together.

Step one and two in recovery are:

1. Realize you are powerless over your struggle or issue and that your life has become unmanageable.
2. You've come to believe that a power greater than yourself can restore you to sanity.

Believe it or not, this is the best place to start. No ego, no agenda, just a mess of jumbled up hurt that feels impossible to get through. While forgiveness may seem too difficult a task for you, with help it can be achieved. This is a promise straight from my lips to your heart.

With help, even the most deep-seated heart wounds that are full of scar tissue can not only be healed, but can also be completely renewed and restored. It's time to stop denying the pain and start realizing that you can't do this on your own...you need help.

When I first started searching for a way through my hurt, I read every book on the topic of forgiveness that I could get my hands on. Yet at the time, I was unable to receive or internalize any wisdom or truth in those books for one simple reason—I hadn't allowed my heart wound to be properly cared for first.

It didn't take long for me to realize that I had missed a pivotal step in the healing process. What I needed first and foremost for my broken heart was comfort. I could not receive truth, or in any way heal, because my wounded heart needed first aid...first.

Believe it or not, timing plays an integral part in healing. There is a time to forgive but it must be preceded by a time to receive comfort for our wounds. I believe this is the number one reason many of us find it impossible to heal from our hurts. Our wounds have not been properly comforted and cared for. We need a time to be broken-hearted in order to forgive. This is a step that cannot be skipped.

Today, my friend, is the time to be brokenhearted. The time to forgive will come.

The medical world understands that when we are wounded and hurting, the very first thing needed to treat that wound is first aid. For heart wounds, this first aid comes in the form of comfort and care.

Getting the right comfort for our heart wounds is necessary for us to heal properly. In the medical field, the first thing to do when treating an injury is to administer first aid. Stop the bleeding—treat the wound – stabilize the patient.

By definition, first aid means: to provide initial assistance, to start with support.

Timing is so important when caring for the wounds of the broken-hearted. This is a first things first scenario. We must start with seeking support, comradery and assistance when our hearts are wounded.

Also, on the flip side—we must be willing to offer aid in the form of support and assistance to others who are struggling with a wounded heart.

We live in a world that tells us to 'hurry up and heal'. After all, it makes us uncomfortable to be around someone who is wounded, especially if there isn't anything we can do to fix it.

Often, it's that uncomfortableness with being around someone with a heart wound that leads us to give unsolicited advice or counsel, rather than comfort and care.

How many of us can just sit and grieve with those who are hurting? No words, just be there next to them while they grieve.

The time for truth, advice and counsel will come later. First, we must support and assist the brokenhearted.

That statement beckons the question, "when is the right time to share the truth about the importance of forgiveness?" While that may not be an easy question to answer I can assure you, the correct answer IS NOT immediately after the injury has occurred.

Timing is defined as: Judgment of when to act, the ability to choose, or the choice of the best moment to do or say something.

Allow me to share a few examples of bad timing in the form of good advice at the wrong time:

- Telling a recent widow that their loved one is in a better place.
- Speaking the words, "well, it could be worse...at least you didn't experience (fill in the blank).
- Quoting a Bible verse on forgiveness to someone who has a fresh heart wound.

The day after I had discovered all of my husband's secrets, I picked up the phone and called the pastor of my church. Through a sea of tears, I shared with him that my heart had been broken and that I didn't know what I was going to do.

Here I was, in my moment of greatest need, searching for a morsel of support and care from this man of God. Unfortunately, what came at me from the other side of the phone was a poorly timed Bible verse on the topic of forgiveness.

He told me that I needed to be like Jesus and forgive my husband not just once, but 70x7 times. I could not believe my ears as I quickly tried to do the math in my head...THAT'S 490 times! Are you saying I should forgive my husband's infidelity, immediately and continually? I was stunned.

It felt like he had just thrown salt into my wounds. When I hung up the phone, not only did I feel like a failure as a wife, because I couldn't keep my husband from straying...but now I also felt like a failure in my faith because I couldn't simply forgive.

I have personally experienced this type of 'support' many times. Words of wisdom and advice are usually offered with the best of intentions. Yet they can harm more than help, primarily due to the timing of when they are shared.

One should never tell a recent widow that 'all things work together for good'. Losing a spouse is hard, and while those words may be considered ultimate truth by many, sharing them at the wrong time is wounding.

We all know this world is full of troubles and heartache. Thankfully, there are resources to help get us through our troubles. It took me years to get the help I needed. What I didn't need was someone's opinion or advice—at least not at first. I needed first and foremost to find comfort for my wounded heart.

In the next few chapters, we'll unpack and dive deep into the topic of finding comfort for our wounds. This is often an overlooked yet necessary step in the healing process. I believe that skipping this step is what causes the most damage in our lives.

Chapter 2
My Story – Part 2

My first memory as a child is one that in many ways defines me. This one incident was pivotal in not only molding my nature, but it also played a part in setting my personality.

I was just a baby at the time, still sleeping in a crib, maybe around two years of age. Yet this single event seared into my subconscious and has since impacted my behavior in many ways.

My mother had just placed me in the crib for the night, when suddenly her brother (my uncle) burst into the room and violently attacked her. He was intent on killing her. It took four family members and several minutes to pry his hands from her throat. The ambulance came to take my mother to the hospital and the police came to take my uncle to jail.

They were both drunk yet that is not what made this event so memorable. Drinking, drugging and violence were the norm in my childhood household. What distinguished this memory was how I reacted to it. I distinctly recall pretending to be asleep through all the commotion. I remember thinking that if I just kept my eyes closed and my mouth shut then maybe my uncle wouldn't notice that I was in the room, and he wouldn't try to hurt me.

That, 'hide-so-they-wont-see-me' behavior was how I coped with every stressful situation as a child and well into adulthood. Why didn't I cry or scream instead of pretending to be asleep? Would my mother have been rescued sooner? I guess we'll never know.

Fighting was my parents' primary way of communicating. They fought so often that the police were called to our home several times a week and they knew us by name. They would break up the fight, pat us kids on the head, and leave. Often only to return hours later, or (on a good week) a few days later.

My mother was always the instigator. She would coerce my father into her unstable world by bombarding him with a constant stream of accusations and obscenities until he would eventually give in and engage in her sick desire to get attention and create drama.

Mom was unstable to say the least. Diagnosed with schizophrenia, she was extremely manic. One day she would be the life of the party. The next, we would find her lying in a bathtub of blood after trying to kill herself—again. The scar tissue on her wrists was over an inch thick. The doctors got so fed up with stitching her up that they would encourage her and even show her the 'right way' to cut herself in order to end her life.

Every morning when my dad left for work, he told us that it was our job to hide the alcohol from our mother. She always had ways to find it and would stop at nothing to coerce us into telling her where it was hidden. It was a daily game of cat and mouse. We (her children) were her victims. Being bit, pinched, burned with cigarettes, and yelled at, daily.

Addiction was a verb in my household and not just in the singular sense. Many compulsions spurred my parents into a diversity of dependence on one thing or another, often multiplying upon themselves.

My mother's abuse varied based on two primary things:

1. Her mood that day, and
2. The amount of alcohol she had consumed.

She was a mean drunk. On her best days she was able to enjoy life, and fun was her middle name. On her good days this woman had a playfulness about her that was both undeniable and wonderful to behold.

Other days the abuse was just verbal. A constant reminder of how awful her life was and how unhappy she was with her marriage, her children, and how she desired to end her existence.

Then there were the days when she would fly off the handle and physically abuse us. Excusing her violent behavior by making sure to tell us that we deserved to be bitten, hit, or burned with cigarettes.

She often reminded us that we should be grateful that she didn't have an abortion when she was pregnant. I was in my thirties the last time she said that to me. I didn't know how to respond. Should one say, "thanks mom for choosing life?" Does Hallmark carry a greeting card that could express my gratitude?

I was around seven years old when my parents divorced. The courts awarded my mother custody of us four children, even though we had told them that we preferred to live with our dad.

My Story – Part 2

Within weeks mom decided she could not handle us any longer, so she locked us in the car and called our father to come get us.

My dad did his best to raise us. We were not easy children. As a newly single father of four, he was desperate for help. At first, he hired nannies to care for us. Some would stick around for a few weeks, others only a few hours. Within a years' time, Dad had remarried, and we had a new 'mom'.

Dad was handsome and charming, and most women found him irresistible. While my mother brought out the worst in him, he was generally a gentle, kind and likable person. Yet with one major weakness...women.

The way it translated in my young mind was that his women were always more important to him than his children. He was a good provider and always kept a roof over our heads and food on the table, but there was always the general unspoken understanding that we (his children) were his burden to bear.

As the oldest girl in the family, I was far beyond my years in maturity. I naturally became my father's defender, caretaker and cheerleader. My young mind reasoned that the best way to show devotion to my father was to become what he most needed.

While women constantly came in and out of our lives, I was consistent in my love and care for this man. Soon he started referring to me as his 'rock'. This made me feel significant and loved.

I quickly learned that significance came in the form of rescuing, helping and fixing others.

Dad was an all-around addict. He didn't play favorites when it came to addiction. He drank heavily, drugged often and partied as much as humanly possible. Yet none of that mattered to me because he needed and depended on me.

Who else was going to care for him when he passed out on the floor with the drug needle still stuck in his arm? Who else was going to call in sick for him when he was too stoned or hungover to get out of bed?

Dad's addictions grew, as addictions do, so much so that I never knew who or what I would come home to. Every morning, I woke up unsure if he had come home the night before or even if he was still alive.

Over time I began to hate his lifestyle—all the while fiercely defending him.

Eventually, that lifestyle caught up with him and he lost everything. Today I am happy to say that he is clean and sober.

After my parents' divorce, my mother was in and out of my life. She would spend a few years sober but eventually her love for alcohol would rear its ugly head and take over.

She was 54 years old when she passed away. In her last year of life, she lived on cigarettes and alcohol. She stopped eating food in order to maintain her figure while drinking heavily. ALL of her daily caloric intake came from booze. Yet it wasn't the drinking that killed her, it was the smoking. She passed away a few months after being diagnosed with lung cancer.

It was my parents' lifestyle that fueled my passion to grow up and one day be a homemaker and mother. In high school my greatest accomplishment was as the proud president of 'Future Homemakers of America'. I was determined to do whatever it took to have what I refer to as a—*white picket fence life.*

My Story – Part 2

I first met my husband in the 9th grade, and we hit it off right away. Not as boyfriend and girlfriend but as good friends. He was outgoing, smart, and most importantly, funny. It didn't matter what was going on at home because I always knew when I got to school, he would make me laugh and feel better. We were best friends throughout high school but never dated until our senior year.

It did not take long for romance to blossom. We spent every spare minute together during our senior year of High School and we grew closer each day. By the time we graduated, I was planning my wedding. I married my best friend one year out of High School and I could not have been more excited about starting a life with this man.

Married life was good, for the most part. Not great, but good...for a few years at least. We would argue about the typical things—sex and money. But since we didn't really have any money, we mostly argued about sex. He wanted more, and I was too tired.

With my marriage being far from ideal, I quickly adopted my mother's marriage creed. She would often say, "if he's not beating or cheating, you shouldn't be bleating." Mom religiously believed and practiced this dogma, and it was her primary criterion for being in a relationship.

I would try to convince myself that I was living a fairy tale. That white picket fence life I always dreamed about. I guess I just thought it would be different to this.

Four years into our marriage, that fairy tale became a nightmare, when my knight in shining armor confessed to an affair.

I had known for some time that he was not happy, as he had once or twice suggested we go to marriage counseling. Yet at the time I dismissed his feelings and instead assured him that our struggles were simply normal growing pains in any young marriage.

In hindsight, the signs were all there. But just as I did as a baby, I chose to ignore the obvious, pull the proverbial covers over my eyes as I pretended to be asleep. That way I wouldn't get hurt.

That affair forced me to open my eyes. It also kicked into gear my codependency. At first, I begged my husband not to leave me. I promised to do and be anything he wanted just so long as he didn't leave.

He was impressed by my plea and agreed to see a counselor to see if we could salvage our marriage. In our first meeting, she shared something that would turn my entire world upside down.

After spending just one hour with us, she told me that my husband had never been faithful to me. She explained that he had always cheated on our marriage by making something else more important —his job, the newest hobby of that week, working out, going out with his friends. There was always something that came before his wife. Only, I didn't pay attention until it was another woman.

I left her office feeling stunned, like I had been sucker-punched. That was the beginning of an awakening for me, and a few days later I had a newfound strength.

I didn't deserve this treatment! My husband's behavior was not right, and I should not put up with infidelity! As reality flooded in, I became more and more angry. Within a week I decided that I needed some space to sort things out, so I left with our two-year-old son.

Four months later, I felt ready to work on our marriage again and my husband moved back into our home. He agreed to doing things such as, going to church and marriage counseling, traveling less for work, and prioritizing our family.

We found a church, started counseling, and I immediately got pregnant with our second child. Getting pregnant was definitely not the plan as I had taken precautions to avoid it.

Now I had not one but two reasons to try and make our marriage work—our children. I became more determined than ever to do whatever it took to break our generational family legacy of divorce.

All our efforts helped, and for a while I thought that life could not get much better. I constantly strived to strengthen our marriage by reading books, taking seminars and classes, as well as continued counseling. I had convinced myself that my marriage was now healed and stronger than ever.

What I didn't see was reality, and that reality was soon to be dragged into the light. There were things which had been hidden in darkness for many years and the universe decided that it was time to make themselves known. Whether it be karma, the universe, or a higher power, I believe something supernatural decided that it was time for my husband's secrets to be exposed.

That day of discovery is forever burned into my memory. The day that my husband's life-long sex addiction could no longer be kept a secret or hidden from my sight. It was time for him to come completely clean. The evidence could not be disputed. He had been caught.

What I did not know at that time was that what I had discovered was just the tip of the iceberg. It took several days for all his secrets to come to light.

I was devastated. Heartbroken. How could I possibly stay in my marriage now? My internal voice told me that no one in their right mind would, especially considering the years of lies, secrets and betrayal. My thoughts kept telling me that I did not deserve this, and that it wasn't fair. Like a record on repeat in my head. I could see no other choice than divorce.

Yet how was I to tell our children? My heart broke as I looked into their wounded, confused eyes, and explained that daddy had broken the rules in our marriage and had to move out. It was more than my heart could bear. Seeing them process their father moving out felt like cutting at my heart wounds with a dull, rusty knife.

I tried to be strong, but witnessing the devastation in my children's eyes made me question everything. For a moment I pondered whether I could pretend that everything was okay. Could denial or ignoring the situation be a viable solution? Can one be plugged back into the matrix once the truth is out? Could I just go back to living in blissful ignorance?

As our family sat in the living room surrounded by sadness, I felt compelled to assure our children that their dad and I would do whatever we could to try and keep our family together.

I began to force myself to consider this marriage separation as a potential means to recovery and restoration, rather than divorce.

I convinced myself that if I just assumed the role of being the supportive wife of an addict, maybe this would be easier. I told myself that if I could just find a way to get through the pain, and process the betrayal, then maybe I could use my hurt to help others. Then it would be worth it.

These mind games gave me hope to see a greater purpose in all this brokenness. In hindsight, what I really wanted was to rush the healing part so that I could hurry up and get to the helping others part.

What I didn't understand was that this type of healing cannot be rushed. I waited and waited for my husband to get fixed. I did all I could think of to heal my hurts, so that we could move on with our lives.

Eventually my waiting became discouragement, and that discouragement turned to frustration. Over time my frustration became anger and let me tell you—anger slammed hard into my life! Like a light switch, I became mad. I was mad at my husband. I was mad at the universe, and I was mad at whatever higher power was out there.

What I didn't realize was that undealt with anger becomes bitterness. Now bitterness had become my addiction. I couldn't let go of it, not that I didn't try. I would set my mind and will to letting go of the hurts so that I could forgive and move on, and it would work for a day or two. But then something would remind me of the betrayal or trigger a memory and I'd immediately catapult right back to that pit of bitterness.

When it came to my marriage, I became suspicious about everything. Every phone call, every lunch meeting, every business trip, every dollar spent. That suspicion quickly became obsession as I was determined to catch my husband doing wrong or bad things.

Many hours were spent snooping, digging, setting traps—seeking any evidence that would convict him. I often counted the money in his wallet and would scour through the credit card charges. Of course, I peppered him with accusations daily.

Being consumed with fear and living in constant suspicion began to change how I looked at my husband. The same man I spoke the words, 'until death do us part' to—I now had utter disdain for. Eventually that disdain grew into full on disgust, and I found myself hating this man more and more, every day.

It is important to understand that all the while I was active in my bitterness, I was also diligent in seeking help. In the four years I spent spiraling out of control, I faithfully went to counseling and recovery meetings, I met with accountability partners, led Bible study groups and often sought spiritual counsel. I volunteered for several non-profits. I spent more time 'working on myself', while actively living in bitterness, than I have at any other time in my life.

I knew it was wrong to be so unforgiving and hateful, but I was stuck. I didn't know how not to be bitter or even if I really wanted to not be bitter. Holding onto the hurts gave me a sense of control and strength that I had never experienced before. I liked this new me that didn't put up with getting taken advantage of or walked all over. I refused to be the timid, ignorant wife of my youth—now I was a bad bitch and my husband knew it.

At the same time, I could not see the harm that unforgiveness and bitterness was doing. Not only in my marriage, but in my body and in all my relationships. My friends started avoiding me, my children lived in constant limbo not knowing if mom and dad were going to stay together or get divorced. Yet it all just seemed like sweet justice to me. I had convinced myself that my husband deserved every bit of my anger, resentment, and bitterness. I'd tell myself that I just needed new friends.

At one point, things had gotten so bad and seemed so hopeless that my husband and I sought out yet another marriage counselor with the hopes that maybe it would somehow help our relationship this time around.

Within a few weeks, she started bringing up the topic of forgiveness and I would just shut down. I didn't want to talk about my unforgiveness. I wanted to focus on the things that my husband needed to work on and change.

My unforgiveness was so strongly rooted at that point that our marriage counselor began to counsel us to prepare ourselves for yet another separation. Not because there was another betrayal or more lies, but for the simple fact that I just was not able to forgive and let go of the hurt so we could start to heal.

Several months into our weekly meetings with her, she asked to meet with me alone. Entering her office, I fully expected her to tell me that it was time to move on and get a divorce. I was not expecting to hear her words that day...

She shared that from what she could see, I was now the reason my marriage was in shambles. She said that if I were to die that day, I would be held accountable for the unhealthiness of my marriage, not my husband! Since I refused to change, or more importantly forgive, I was hurting the marriage. She asked me to give her counsel a few days to 'soak in', and she made me promise that I would not make any rash decisions based on our conversation. I left her office feeling stunned—sucker punched by her words. As I drove home, I found myself overwhelmed by the unfairness of it all. It felt so wrong for her to blame me. After all, I had never betrayed the marriage. How could she place any of the blame on me? How dare she!

When I got home, I locked myself in the bedroom and sobbed on the floor for hours. I felt desperate, lost, discouraged and hopeless. I pleaded with the universe to give me something, anything, to help me figure out how to move past my bitterness so that I could let go and get on with my life. I knew my behavior was doing a lot of damage, but I just didn't know how to stop.

That same day, I believe there was some type of divine intervention. Something in the universe heard my cries and that higher power responded to my plea for help. Once I had cried all my tears, I sat up, looked around and noticed my Bible on the nightstand. Something prompted me to open it, so I laid it on my lap and let it just fall open—wishing in my heart for a 'genie in a bottle' kind of moment. Searching for any words that could help me right then.

Believe it or not, this book fell open at Psalms 55 to a story of a man who was betrayed by a life-long companion. This man (David) says that when a close friend betrays us, it hurts so much more than when a stranger hurts us. He goes on to describe the intense pain that is felt when the one who does the betraying is a companion.

As I read this story it felt like a lightbulb turned on in my head and in my heart. This might sound crazy, but I truly believe there was a supernatural, intentional intervention that happened that day. Reading that story spoke directly to my heart. I could feel hope and adrenaline shooting into my weary soul.

Somehow, it felt like I had just been given the answer to my life struggle. After all the times I searched for answers from books, counselors, spiritual leaders and friends, these were the words I needed to hear at the exact moment I needed to hear them. Here it was—plain and simple. Presented to me like a long overdue gift...

I needed to give my hurts to someone or something outside of my person. I needed to trust that the universe had a plan for the hurt

I'd experienced. I should understand that while I may not be able to see that plan, I needed to trust the process.

Holding onto my hurts was only causing more hurt. Letting go of them just didn't work for me. But giving them to someone or something who can better deal with them...that felt good and right—healthy and hopeful.

Suddenly I found myself whispering, "I'm going to give my hurts to my higher power to deal with. I'm going to trust that there is something out there bigger than I, that can handle my bitterness better than I."

There it was—my Mecca. I had finally found the key to unlocking this prison of resentment and bitterness. That day I wrote in my journal, "Today I struggle with my resentment and anger, and something brought me to Psalm 55 in the bible. Help me to trust in my higher power. May this be a turning point in my ability to forgive!"

That moment became my turning point.

That day I found the solution to my unforgiveness and bitterness and that day I started to change. I began letting go of my hurts and trusting the universe to handle the rest.

For some ,the 'universe' may be something like a higher power. Think of it as where you place your faith. For others, giving their hurts to the universe may involve seeking outside help such as psychiatry or meditation. It's personal and individual, yet we all must get to a place where we reach for guidance outside of our own selves and trust that there is a bigger plan.

Believe it or not, my heart almost immediately started changing. And just one month after I had that moment of enlightenment, I revisited that same journal entry and penned these words next to my original ones:

> *"Today I am grateful. My higher power has been faithful! I think I've finally figured out how to forgive."*

I'm in awe of the miracle performed in my heart and mind, and even in my marriage. My tattered old heart wasn't just healed, but I've been given a new heart—especially towards my husband.

I am so grateful to be able to say that not only do I love my husband today, but I also actually like him. If you knew how stuck I was in unforgiveness before, you would understand how huge it is to now say I like my husband. And that's not all, there's more...I enjoy spending time with my husband. But most miraculous of all, I look forward to growing old with him. Do you hear the angels singing? This is a freakin miracle!

Now let me assure you, this process of figuring out how to forgive has not been easy in any way at all. But I will say (and would shout it if I thought it would help get the point across) that figuring out how to forgive has 100 percent been worth it!

I see now that my unforgiveness only hurt me. This journey has taught me how to trust the painful (yet necessary) process of getting past a hurt. I am grateful for the lessons I've learned and the mistakes I've made because they have gotten me to where I am today. I am confident that regardless of what the future holds for me, I will never again struggle with unforgiveness or bitterness in quite the same way or at the same level that I once did.

Sometimes the hardest lessons are the ones that teach us the most.

My Story – Part 2

There you have it—the highlights and lowlights of my life story. I wanted to share it with you for several reasons:

First, I hope you understand that I know how it feels to be hurt to the deepest core of being. Next, I want to share the lessons learned from my many attempts (and fails) at trying to forgive. And finally, I'd like to walk you through my personal steps of getting to forgiveness.

So many times I was told that I just needed to 'choose to forgive and forgive'. I tried to will it, but it just never worked for me...I needed more. I needed a step-by-step guide on how to get from A to B. That is what I hope to give you in this book.

One thing I've learned is that transparency is key to healing. As you've probably already deduced, I am someone who has chosen to be completely open about my hurts, issues, and struggles. I believe we can all benefit from learning how to forgive in a healthier way.

First, we must find comfort for our broken heart. Next, we need to understand that there are consequences to harboring unforgiveness, resentment and bitterness. Finally, we need to acquire the tools to manage our minds on a daily basis so that unforgiveness doesn't try to creep back in.

There are many things that will try to convince us to hold onto our hurts and keep them safely hidden, deep down. We work hard at never letting others know those hurts are there. We go through our daily lives believing the lie that exposing our hurt is a sign of weakness. In truth our hurts need to come into the light in order to heal.

Living life as an open book has been a huge leap of faith for me. I grew up in a home that was shrouded in secrecy and shame, so learning to be authentic and transparent has been challenging to say the least. But realizing that my higher power already knows my imperfections, struggles, failures and even the most embarrassing, humiliating things about me, has made me question why I was expending so much energy trying to hide these things from others?

Now, I want to be clear about what I am saying and I'm not saying here. I'm not saying that we should be willing to walk up to any stranger on the street and share our deepest, darkest secrets. Not at all. Most of us know someone who probably couldn't keep a confidence if it killed them. And then there are those who are always on the lookout for any juicy piece of gossip that they can use against us. They're definitely out there. I'm not advocating or encouraging you to start revealing every intimate detail about your life to anyone within earshot.

What I want you to hear is that we all need someone in our lives who we can confide in. Some of us (like myself) feel comfortable sharing quite a bit of their lives with the general public, while others may not. That's okay. There can be different levels and different types of confidants in our lives, but the fact remains that we need someone to confide in. Why? Well one primary reason is; secrets make us sick.

Another reason we need someone to confide in is because; the truth sets us free. Whether it's knowing a truth or telling a truth. They both can and will set us free!

Are you ready to be totally transparent and completely authentic in your life? Maybe not to the whole world, but to someone you can trust? If so, what will that look like? If not, what is holding you back?

Take my hand and let's start this forgiveness journey together. I promise it will be worth it!

Chapter 3
Where do we start?

So how and where do we start this forgiveness process? What's it going to take to receive a supernatural healing from our hurts? Thankfully there is only one simple criterion necessary to start this process—only one obligation that you must fulfill in order to begin the restoration process that leads back to health.

And what is that one thing you ask? **FAITH**

Faith is defined as: *belief in, devotion to, or trust in somebody or something, especially without logical proof.*

There you have it. How simple is that? You just need to have faith in the process. How much faith, you ask? Just enough to keep learning the steps while you trust the process.

You may notice that one of my favorite books is the dictionary. I love looking up the definition of a word. The English language can have so many different meanings for a single word. Often the true definition can get lost, and therefore rediscovered. I find the dictionary to be a back-to-basics tool that usually helps me keep things simple, clear and real.

That being said, let's look at the definition of 2 imperative words to this study:

Ministering: *to attend to the wants and needs of others.*

Comfort: *to soothe, console, reassure.*

When our hearts are wounded and we want to heal, it's imperative that we experience being attended to. We all need comfort for our downcast spirit.

Think about a child who slips and scrapes his or her knee. Our first reaction is to comfort them. Maybe we embrace them and kiss their boo-boo (if they are itty bitty ones). And then only after we've put way too many band aids on the tiny scratch, do we discuss how it was not a good idea to run around the pool, or how they need to hold onto the stair rail while walking up or down the stairs.

It is our nature to comfort those who are suffering from a physical injury. As a society, we intentionally care for those who are mourning the loss of a loved one. Yet for some reason it can be challenging to comfort those suffering from a betrayal. Maybe because we don't know what to say or maybe we personalize the situation and think about what we would do if we were in their situation. Unfortunately, we often offer things like unsolicited advice, opinions and judgments, rather than comfort.

If you've been brokenhearted, I'm willing to bet that you've probably been given a lot of opinions, advice and judgment about what you should (or should not) do.

Notice that comfort is NOT defined as giving advice or offering opinions.

I've had so many give their opinions, offer advice and make well-meaning comments that came off as judgments:

Some examples of opinions and/or advice that I've received:

"You should separate." "You should divorce."

"You should separate, but not divorce because God hates divorce." "You should read this book."

"You just need to pray about it."

"You should really get some counseling."

"You should NOT talk to your husband." "You SHOULD talk to your husband."

"Maybe if you worked, your husband would respect you more and not treat you that way."

Some of the judgment I received:

"I'd never tolerate that kind of treatment."

"My loved one would never do something like that." "Well, it takes two to make a broken relationship." "You know, we teach others how to treat us."

Or how about those looks that seem to say:

"You're weak. Why would you allow those things to happen to you?" "You're naive. What makes you think things will ever change?"

"You're flawed. Something must be wrong with you otherwise he wouldn't have strayed." The list could go on and on...

I'm going to go out on a limb and make a bold statement here.

It seems to me that unsolicited advice is generally interpreted as correction or condemnation. Rarely is it received as comfort.

Correction is usually cruelty unless preceded with comfort.

Sadly, I received more judgment, advice and criticism from people who were considered 'religious'. I know it may be hard to believe, but it's the truth. After my heartbreak I sought out my non-religious friends for comfort and support. They were better at understanding my situation and empathizing with my struggle. For the most part they validated me without telling me what I should do, and they listened without giving advice.

From the beginning, many of my religious friends counseled me to forgive. While I believe they spoke the truth, their timing was off. What I needed first and foremost for my broken heart was comfort (remember the definition of comfort: to sooth, console, reassure).

I realize that not everyone who is stuck in unforgiveness can relate to my experience of feeling unsupported by my religious community. Some of you may not have experienced a lack of comfort or support and have actually had the opposite.

To be honest, I considered omitting those paragraphs because they may only pertain to a select few. Yet as I began to share my experience with others and in turn hear theirs, the stories of people feeling misunderstood, criticized and judged were undeniable and almost universal.

You're not alone. Healing requires feeling connected to others who have had similar experiences. Knowing you are not alone ***is*** (in and of itself) comforting.

Where do we start?

For those of you who have religious friends that have comforted you in a way that has truly helped you heal, I just want to shout—hurray! Seriously, do you know how blessed you are? Please thank them. You are well on your way to true healing. May these next few pages be like icing on your comfort cake.

On the other hand, if you've felt that need for comfort has been overlooked then my hope for you is that these next few pages will shower you with an abundance of supernatural care. May the words I share be a soothing ointment for your neglected wounds.

That day when I opened my Bible to the chapter in Psalms, the words literally leaped off the page. This man, King David, felt exactly how I was feeling. He knew the pain of being betrayed by a close friend, a trusted companion.

David says in Psalm 55:12-14 that he could endure it if an enemy was insulting (or betraying) him, but then he goes on to say that when it's someone he trusted who betrays him, the wounds hurt more. Here are those same words from a different translation:

> *This isn't the neighborhood bully mocking me—I could take that. This isn't a foreign devil spitting invective—I could tune that out. It's you! We grew up together! You! My best friend! Those long hours of leisure as we walked arm in arm...and this, my best friend, betrayed his best friends; his life betrayed his word. All my life I've been charmed by his speech, never dreaming he'd turn on me. His words, which were music to my ears, turned to daggers in my heart.*
> (Psalm 55:12-14; 20-21)

King David was a gallant warrior and brilliant military leader who led his nation into a time of its greatest power. He was Israel's most celebrated king. Yet he also had a sensitive side as he was a poet and a musician. Sounds like the perfect man wouldn't you say? He sure was impressive on paper.

Sadly, as great as David looked on paper, he was far from perfect. His long list of indiscretions and flat out wrong doings included things such as adultery and murder.

I found it so comforting to discover that someone like this—a warrior king, someone strong, smart, who loved passionately, could feel what I was feeling. This man had a deeply spiritual side to him, yet simultaneously experienced feelings of deep sorrow and gut-wrenching despair. Oddly, I found that very validating.

It also reassured me to read how this man was *so confident* in his relationship with his higher power, that he felt safe enough to express his feelings **and** his faith **simultaneously**. I never thought that was allowed, that was a new concept for me.

My parents rarely, (if ever) went to church. My mother would often say that the walls would collapse if she ever dared enter any religious building. The only time I ever attended Church as a child was when I visited my grandparents, or if a friend of our family offered to pick me up and take me.

My grandparents were from a generation that believed the only feelings you should **ever** mix with your faith were the *fruit of the spirit* feelings: love, joy, peace, patience, kindness, goodness, gentleness, faithfulness and self-control. Negative feelings were wrong and therefore sin, especially when expressed to a holy higher power. It was a HUGE no-no to complain to anyone.

Where do we start?

Our family motto was...

Any ill will or unhappy emotions were to be promptly swept under a rug.

Growing up, church was where we would go to pretend. I enjoyed playing make-believe because it allowed me to (for a moment) imagine that I had a normal, happy family life.

Every week, I escaped reality for a few short hours while I sat in a church pew. It didn't matter if all hell was breaking loose at home (and it usually was) because for those precious few moments, I got to act like all was well in my little pretend world.

Imagine my surprise to discover that someone like this person (King David), who believed and had faith in a higher power, also complained to Him?

This person had mood swings just like me? He had good days and bad days? He got angry at the powers that be, and complained when he was hurt or upset? WOW!

Here are just a few of the words King David spoke, directly to his higher power:

> *"How long must I wrestle with my thoughts and day after day have sorrow in my heart? How long will my enemy triumph over me?"*—Psalm 13:2

> *"Long enough, God—you've ignored me long enough. I've looked at the back of your head long enough. Long enough I've carried this ton of trouble, lived with a stomach full of pain. Long enough my arrogant enemies have looked down their noses at me."*—Psalm 12:2 MSG

I've asked the question "how long must I suffer?" More times than I can count.

The point here is that this man knew what broken heartedness felt like. He was familiar with being tormented by his thoughts. He was a man who intimately knew and loved his higher power with all his heart, *yet He still questioned him at times.*

My heart wounds caused me to question **everything**...down to my core beliefs. I was tormented with thoughts and emotions that ranged from feeling insecure about my decisions, to questioning the purpose and plan for my life. At times I even questioned the existence of a higher power. I was plagued with a feeling that I was expendable and unimportant to the universe. It felt as though I didn't matter. Was I just a tool to be used and then tossed away like trash?

What if my purpose was to be used as an instrument and then cast aside? **What if** my life didn't really matter? **What if** my higher power loved others more than me? **What if** my purpose in life was to experience broken heartedness and that's all there is?

If only my higher power could go back and change the past and stop my husband before he betrayed me. **If only** my higher power would tell me what I should do next and confirm whether I'm making the right decisions. **If only** this supernatural power would insert Himself into my life and clean up this mess.

Now I know that those statements may seem extreme, but I also know that many who go through the sufferings of a broken heart have questioned their purpose in life. My mind knew the truth (that there was a plan and a purpose, and my higher power could be trusted) yet my heart tormented me with all the **what if's** and **if only's...**

Where do we start?

At times, we all struggle with thoughts and feelings that torment us. And we all have times when we are consumed with the 'what if' and 'if only' scenarios.

I hope you find comfort in knowing that you are not alone in how you are feeling or what you are thinking. There is no shame in it, only truth, comradery and ultimately freedom through the process. Just keep hanging on and hanging in there...it will get better, I promise!

King David is just one example of someone who communicates with such honesty, transparency and rawness. And he invites us to sit next to him on this roller coaster ride of emotions as he expresses things such as: Joy, excitement, compassion, love, anger, sorrow, depression (just to name a few).

Have you ever felt like society encourages you to sugar coat your situation?

We may catch ourselves saying or thinking things like, "this is really hard, but I know it is for my own good so I'll just grin and bear it." Or, "I just need to fake it till I make it."

We convince ourselves that help is available, just as soon as we change our attitude.

This is just not true. Your higher power is not waiting for you to get a better attitude. In fact, we need to cry out *IN OUR DISTRESS*. If we are angry at the powers that be for allowing this hurt to happen, or for not protecting us from the hurt, *we should feel that fully*. Your higher power can handle it.

Here's a letter I wrote to God on August 24, 2003, sharing how I was feeling.

> *I wandered through the Bible again, in search of comfort this morning. The night was filled with nightmares, and I awoke feeling desperate for peace. I was surprised at what I found and this morning I am grateful.*
> *For a moment, I have been given relief from my sorrow and while I'm sure it's short lived, right now I feel comforted.*
> *I am reminded that I can trust in my higher power and that is my heart's desire. I need to look to you as my helper, God. I suppose I should have been doing that all along.*
> *While I don't see a way out of this pain, I am grateful for the short reprieves from it.*
> *I'm not really sure what these hurts want to teach me. Maybe I am just a tool to be used and then tossed aside? Am I expendable—just a pawn in this game of life? Did I do, or not do, something to deserve this? Am I upsetting you with all my complaining? Am I so shallow that I can't even trust that there may be bigger things happening outside of my understanding? What is wrong with me?!*
> *I ask that these bad dreams be taken away. Nights are the worst. The universe must know I'm most vulnerable at night.*

I hope you know that no matter what you say to your higher power, they can handle it. They are not judging you for being upset or angry about what's happened to you. If you've been hurt by someone you trusted, *it's okay to be upset*! If you've been betrayed by someone who was supposed to protect you, *it's okay to say that it doesn't seem fair.*

Where do we start?

I hope you have been given a clear understanding that you are not alone in your suffering. There are those who want to help you by attending to and caring for your broken heart. Something bigger and greater than you, can and will help to relieve and ease the pain you're going through. You just have to trust the process...and read on!

Chapter 4
The benefits of being brokenhearted

Does that statement seem like an oxymoron to you? It certainly doesn't seem as though there could be *any* benefits to being brokenhearted. I assure you there are. One in particular is a BIG one! I can't wait to share them with you. In due time, my friend.

First let's look at the definition of that word **brokenhearted**: *To be burdened with great sorrow, grief, or disappointment*

Synonyms of brokenhearted: *heartsick, heartbroken, despondent, dejected.*

Do any of those words (or maybe all of them) describe you?

In my time of great pain, my primary emotion was definitely—*despondent*. I was despondent personified. Extremely unhappy, discouraged and hopeless.

Something I've noticed about brokenheartedness is that our society tends to place it on a scale. For some reason we naturally want to measure our personal pain against other hurtful things.

The benefits of being brokenhearted

It's our nature to compare the weight of our suffering to that of others. Society seems to think that losing a pet might be a two or three on the sadness scale, where a husband betraying or abandoning his family is more like a seven or eight. It's unfathomable to think about what a ten would be on that scale.

I must admit, I'm guilty of this. Comparing my hurts to those of others. In the past when I'd hear someone's story, I'd weigh it against what I've been through. Often having the thought that their pain is nothing compared to mine.

Years ago, a sweet older woman came into my life. She had felt prompted to call me out of the blue to ask how I was doing. We were barely acquaintances. Little did I know we had so much in common. We were both recovering from a broken heart due to a recent marriage betrayal.

This woman has one of the most wise, discerning hearts of anyone I've ever met. Understandably, she quickly became a mentor to me.

The first time she and I sat down to talk, I told her my story and she shared hers. I remember almost immediately thinking that her broken heart was nothing compared to mine; I had her beat by a mile.

Being the wise and discerning woman she is, she somehow sensed me putting our pain on a scale. She then said something that was EXACTLY what I needed to hear. Her words of truth were spoken in gentleness, yet they knocked me right off my little self-constructed pedestal of supreme suffering.

(Yes, that was me, the queen of the broken hearts, supreme in suffering. I think my crown even had teardrop shaped jewels on it)

She ever so gently shared that while the details of our stories are quite different, the hurt is very much the same. Her pain is just as valid and real as mine. Her heart and trust had been shattered, just like mine.

You see, broken-heartedness is just that—brokenheartedness. There are no scales to place it on. It's not about thinking that our pain is more significant than another's. It's okay to be distraught over something that might seem small in comparison to what another person is mourning over.

Pain is personal and unique, and it's not my place (or yours) to judge whether or not it is significant.

I know several people (including close family members) who dearly love their pets and consider them to be their children. Losing a pet would be earth-shatteringly devastating to them.

Whatever the circumstances of your personal heartbreak, I believe there is a custom fitted cast that has been molded perfectly in order to hold all the pieces of your broken heart together so that true healing can begin. The key is to find what comforts you and then allow yourself to be comforted.

Maybe it's your higher power, or God, who comforts you:

> *"You who are my Comforter in sorrow, my heart is faint within me."—Jeremiah 8:18.*

> *"Blessed are those who mourn for they shall be comforted." —Matthew 5:4*

Maybe it's music:

> *"You wear your best apology / But I was there to watch you leave / And all the times I let you in / Just for you to go again."*—Taylor Swift, *The Last Time*

> *"And the tears come streaming down your face. When you lose something you can't replace. When you love someone, but it goes to waste. Could it be worse?"*—Coldplay, *Fix You*

Maybe it's through inspirational reading:

> *"Character cannot be developed in ease and quiet. Only through experience of trial and suffering can the soul be strengthened, ambition inspired, and success achieved."*—Helen Keller

> *"Out of suffering have emerged the strongest souls; the most massive characters are seared with scars."*—Khalil Gibran

Or maybe you receive comfort when in nature:

> *"The best remedy for those who are afraid, lonely or unhappy is to go outside, somewhere where they can be quite alone with the heavens, nature, and God. Because only then does one feel that all is as it should be and that God wishes to see people happy, amidst the simple beauty of nature. As long as this exists, and it certainly always will, I know that then there will always be comfort for every sorrow, whatever the circumstances may be. And I firmly believe that nature brings solace in all troubles."*—Anne Frank

Finding comfort for our heart wounds is so incredibly important to our healing. Suffering will grow within us when we allow it to and when we seek comfort, we will be given the strength to endure the suffering, no matter how long it takes.

Definition of **endure**: *to suffer without yielding; to suffer patiently.*

I hope you feel encouraged to seek and receive comfort, in whatever form best suits you.

It's important to understand that our higher power never *causes* pain to happen in our lives, but they absolutely do allow it. In part because they know that there are benefits to our pain. Our hurts are also an opportunity for us to learn and grow.

Recently a close friend of mine had a miscarriage. This was to be her fourth child, and she and her husband were as excited about this child as they were with their other three. They had already started picking out names. Her oldest was 5 at the time and wanted to name their 3rd child 'baby Hercules'. He was quite upset when mom and dad decided to go in a different direction. The day she found out that this baby was no longer growing inside her, she was unexpectedly calm. She shared the news with her family and friends, and decided that if this was God's will, well then who was she to question it?

But over time, she did start questioning. Why did this have to happen? What could she have done to keep this from happening? Sadly, there were no answers as this had never happened before. Eventually her thoughts shifted and started to change and she wondered if she should even try to have another child. What if this happens again? Will she have to spend her entire pregnancy worried about the health of the baby?

In the midst of our pain, it can be hard to accept comfort in any form. Maybe we wonder why the universe didn't stop the heart wrenching thing from happening to us. If our higher power could have saved us from the pain, why didn't He? Sometimes the comfort offered seems to be too little, too late.

This friend of mine described how she was feeling in such an insightful way. She said it felt like she had been *spiritually bruised.*

Wow! What a clear and profound picture that paints in my mind. What a powerful way to describe how we may feel just after our heart injury.

Think about it...when we are physically bruised, any touch is painful, even if it is intended for comfort. The same is true for those who are spiritually or relationally bruised—even the most loving care can be painful for a time, at least until the bruising goes away.

My friend went on to have more babies. She also spends time walking alongside others who have experienced the same type of loss that she has, offering them comfort, comradery and emotional support. She has used her heartbreak to help others in a way that is incredibly commendable.

That is the *first* benefit that comes with being broken hearted. When we endure suffering and use it to help others, the universe 'commends' us for it.

Commend: *to give special praise to.*

There is a special praise for those who have experienced unjust suffering. It is a blessing that is uniquely ours. We are universally singled out and set apart. We have been gifted the ability to relate to and help others who are hurting.

As a child, I loved playing follow the leader, especially at the beach. I'd follow the footsteps that others had made in the wet sand. I'd make a game of trying to step exactly in each footstep. Sometimes the distance between steps would be too far for my little legs to reach, but I'd do my best to stay exactly in step with the imprints. I know, I'm easily entertained.

Following in someone's footsteps can help us navigate the pain of our heartache, and in turn help us to find some much needed comfort for our heart wounds. It's not a hard thing to do but it does require two important things from us:

1. Trust—we must trust that the person we are following can and will help us.
2. Focus—we must keep our focus on following in another's footsteps right now.

Maybe you're thinking it's just too hard to follow in anyone else's footsteps right now. Once again, I get it, and I've felt that way as well. Thankfully there are many who came before us who are wiser than us and they can encourage us to follow in their footsteps.

The third step in the twelve step Alcoholics Anonymous program states:

> *"We made a decision to turn our will and our lives over to the care of God as we understood Him." "He left his case in the hands of God who always judges fairly."*—1st Peter 2:23 (NIV)

Following in the footsteps of others who came before us is something that is absolutely crucial to figuring out forgiveness. Those two sentences hold the ultimate solution to letting go of all our hurts. They are pure gold!

Trusting our higher power (as we understand him) with our hurts is pivotal to our healing. So critical a thing is it, that I've devoted a few chapters to the topic of trust and surrender, later in this book.

Step 3 in the 12 step recovery process packs a powerhouse punch, reassuring us that our higher power is truly in control. We just need to follow in His footsteps.

Your suffering *is* part of a bigger plan.

I encourage you to go back and read that sentence again. Maybe write it on a note card and put it somewhere so you can read it every time you feel overwhelmed.

Right after my heart was broken, I longed to get even with the one who hurt me. Not that I wanted to go out and do the things that they had done to me, however I certainly entertained ungodly ways to get vengeance more often than I care to admit.

One of my deepest desires was for the person who hurt me to know what it felt like to be on the receiving end of wrongdoing. I wanted them to feel what I was feeling so that they could identify with the pain I was experiencing.

Please understand that my desire to 'get even' was not to punish, seek *revenge*, or retaliate. What I wanted was for them to understand firsthand what they had done to my heart. I wanted them to *empathize* with my suffering.

Let's explore those two words a bit:

Revenge: *the punishment of somebody in retaliation for harm done.*

Empathy: *the ability to identify with and understand somebody else's feelings or difficulties.*

I realize it may be asking too much for the person who hurt me to identify with my feelings or empathize with my pain. Today that is no longer an expectation. It's enough to know that others can identify with what I have been through, and I am not alone.

Now let's discover yet another benefit to brokenheartedness.

> *"He heals the brokenhearted and binds up their wounds."*— Psalm 147:3

The Hebrew word for bind is *chabash* (pronounced, khaw-bash) and it means, 'to wrap firmly, to gird about'. The word 'gird' means to surround something (ie a castle girded with a moat).

I want you to picture your higher power binding up your wounds. Watch as he wraps your broken heart gently yet firmly, surrounding or girding it with His healing touch. He holds the pieces in place with His strong hands.

In my mind my higher power is wearing green medical scrubs, and he is muscular and strong. He assures me that he knows what he's doing, and I have total confidence in Him. He is gentle, yet thorough as he tends to my wounds.

Several years ago we spent 10 days at the beach in southern California. The beach has always been my happy place and I'm not really all that picky regarding what beach. Just plop me near a body of salt water and I'm as happy as a clam.

This particular time, it was our first day of vacation. I was out in the waves, frolicking around with our four kids. Just loving life.

Suddenly I felt something puncture my foot. I instinctively reached down, felt for whatever it was, and promptly plucked it out of my appendage. Turns out it was a large piece of broken glass that had punctured a vein that was now spewing blood everywhere.

Once I attended to the lifeguard, who was about to pass out, we opted to drive to the nearby hospital and get it stitched up. No big deal...or so I thought.

We arrived at the E.R., where they took x-rays to make sure my foot was not broken and there were no foreign objects still stuck in there. Then the doctor began to wash the wound for what seemed like an eternity, just to make sure there were no grains of sand left that could cause an infection.

Then for some odd reason this doctor felt it necessary to warn me to 'brace myself' because he was going to administer a numbing solution in the form of a shot.

He went on to explain that the bottom of the foot is quite thick and calloused, so he would need to go deep with the needle. He also said the part of my foot that needed stitching was VERY sensitive. Later my husband told me that the doctor motioned for him to pin me down, so I couldn't move. Why, you ask?

BECAUSE THIS SHOT HURT LIKE H—E—double toothpicks!

Here I was, a 42 year old mother of four (*hello...I've been through labor and delivery four times—YO!*) I've been stitched in places you don't want a needle anywhere near (if you ladies know what I mean). I can endure this! I laugh in the face of pain. This would be a piece of cake, a walk in the park.

"Bring it on you young, inexperienced, naive little doctor-man."

Bring! It! On!

Well, let me tell you...that little prick of a needle HURT! More than any labor I've ever had. So much so that if I could have, I would have shot up and sucker punched both the doctor and my husband right in the gut (*side note: I'm not a violent person, but I'm a fighter not a fleer. I tend to lash out when scared or in intense pain*).

The only problem with my desire to lash out was that my husband had me pinned down on my stomach so I couldn't move.

Once I realized that there was nothing I could do but endure the pain, I just started to cry. And that tells you how much it really hurt. I rarely cry from physical pain. Earlier that day when I stepped on that evil little devil glass...tear free. Or when my foot was literally gushing blood to the beat of my heart...completely dry eyed.

Once that sadist doctor stitched up my foot, I was released and told that I had to stay out of the water for guess how many days? Ten. The exact number of days we were spending at the beach. I had the stitches removed the same day I got home to beach-less Arizona. What a bummer that trip turned out to be. Talk about being brokenhearted.

I share that story because it makes a crucial point about treating wounds and healing.

Sometimes even the process of caring for our wounds can be intensely painful.

The same can be true for the wounds of the heart. There is rarely painless healing, and oftentimes the process of mending can be *as* painful as, or more painful than the injury itself.

Our higher power promises to care for our wounds and in that sometimes we'll be pinned down for our own good. He won't send a nurse to do the job. He'll stay close to us while we are suffering and will actively be involved in restoring us to health.

Our higher power is in the business of rehabilitation.

Rehabilitate: *to help somebody return to good health and a normal life by providing training and/or therapy.*

The universe provides the training (preparation, teaching, guidance, instruction) and the therapy (treatment, remedy, cure, healing) that you need in order to return to a normal life. What an amazing promise that is.

Now it's time to discover the one really BIG, HUGE in fact, awesome and amazing benefit that is uniquely for the brokenhearted. Are you ready for this? *Cue the cheesy basketball music*

When I discovered this statement I was completely awestruck. It's that good!

> *"The Lord is close to the brokenhearted and he saves those who are crushed in spirit."*—Psalm 34:18

Now I want you to read that from a few other translations. I think it really gives it more meaning and color:

> *"If your heart is broken, you'll find GOD right there. If you're kicked in the gut, he'll help you catch your breath."* (The message Bible)

> *"The LORD is there to rescue all who are discouraged and have given up hope."* (Contemporary English Version)

> *"Near [is] Jehovah to the broken of heart, And the bruised of spirit He saveth."* (Young's Literal Translation)

> *"The LORD is near to those who are discouraged; he saves those who have lost all hope."* (Good New Translation)

What a remarkable verse and statement! We are not alone. Our higher power draws near us in our heartbroken state. And it's spoken as a promise. WOW!

But wait, there's more. I found something truly remarkable about this life changing verse.

Did you know that **the ONLY time the phrase "the Lord is close to" is used in the entire Bible is right here in this verse?** It's true, this is the only time. How amazing is that?

When I first discovered this, I couldn't believe my eyes. I looked up different phrases that meant the same thing, just to see if maybe it was worded differently, but no, there was nothing. The only verse I found that was similar was Psalms 145:18 that says, "the Lord is near to all who call on him, to all who call on him in truth."

But that was it, nowhere else is the phrase "the Lord is close to" used in the entire Bible.

I was amazed, and I hope you find it amazing as well. To read that our higher power uniquely draws "CLOSE" to us in our broken-hearted state is so comforting.

Another word for 'close' is the word 'intimate'.

Our higher power is uniquely close to the brokenhearted, intimately involved in caring for our wounds and monitoring our healing.

Now please understand that by no means am I saying that we should be excited about our brokenheartedness. That would be absurd—and to be honest, a little weird. I think I'd question one's sanity if they went around saying, "Yay, my friend betrayed me!" Or, "I'm so excited that my heart is broken!" That would just be ridiculous.

But, since we can't change the fact that we have been wounded and our hearts are broken or we are crushed in spirit, what better thing to do with our pain than to search for and find the benefits?

Being brokenhearted sucks! There's no two ways around it, but once we accept that we can't change what was done to us, the best thing to do is find a healthy way to get through it.

If you still don't feel the closeness of your higher power...that's okay. Remember, many who came before you also felt abandoned by God. But I'm here to say that God doesn't lie, EVER. So even if you don't feel his closeness right now, the fact is that He *is* close to you in your brokenheartedness. Believe it, accept it, cling to it, because it's truth!

Now let's look closer at the second part of that verse (Psalm 34:18) because it is *equally* amazing: "The Lord is close to the brokenhearted **and saves those who are crushed in spirit."**

Synonyms of **crushed**: *flattened, trampled, trodden.*

Synonyms of **spirit**: *strength, courage, heart, soul.*

What an amazing promise! I hope you can cling to that promise today. Your higher power will rescue those whose hearts are trampled, strength is flattened, soul is trodden.

Who else will draw near to you in your brokenhearted state? In the world, the opposite is often the truth.

The universe will not avoid you when you are suffering. In fact, your higher power will draw intimately close to you as He gently yet firmly binds up the pieces of your broken heart.

If your emotional pain feels like it's too much to bear, try letting your higher power help you!

Chapter 5
Finding Comfort

In the last chapter we learned that in our heartbreak we are uniquely favored by our higher power. If we allow it, that higher power will give us much-needed preferential treatment. He'll care for our crushed spirit in an exclusive way. We are individually singled out and blessed in an exclusive way.

In this chapter, we'll discuss healthy ways to find comfort. The definition that is most fitting for the comfort I am speaking of is: **Relief from pain or anxiety.**

We **all** seek comfort from our pain and anxiety. Every single hurt human will actively search for some sort of reprieve from pain or discomfort. This is a universal truth. Sometimes we find comfort in healthy ways while often we seek and find harmful ways to comfort our wounds. Our nature is to gravitate toward unhealthy sources of comfort such as alcohol, drugs, food, sex, shopping, isolating, etc.

Chances are you've participated in unhealthy ways of seeking comfort at some point in your life. Maybe those roads have led to some scary places that require additional help and therapy.

Maybe instead of seeking comfort, you've chosen to ignore the pain. You figure that if you pay no attention to it, it will just go away. I wish it were so. Unfortunately, denial is no healthier a choice than dependence.

Denial is like an undetected cancer. You can't treat or cure something if you are unable or unwilling to acknowledge it. Denying that you have a hurt that needs to be forgiven is a serious personal problem, and if not dealt with it can wreak havoc in your life.

One of the primary ways unforgiveness and bitterness leak out in our lives is through pain. This could be physical, emotional, mental, relational or spiritual. Pain can range from depression to fatigue and much, much more. Undealt with hurts take their toll on us, one way or another.

A while back my husband and our two sons went to play racquetball. It was on the first serve of their second game that my husband lost his footing on the dusty floor and collapsed. According to our young boys, dad was in a lot of pain because they had 'never seen Dad act like that or talk like that before'.

My husband is a tough guy. He once fractured his femur playing soccer and didn't even know it for weeks. Another time he tore a hamstring while running a marathon and instead of stopping he willed himself to finish the last few miles. That's the kind of crazy, tough guy he is.

But this time, there was no toughing out this injury. He had dislocated his tibia and spiral fractured his fibula. He needed a 6 inch plate with screws surgically placed in his ankle in order to walk again. No wonder our boys had never seen their dad act that way. He had never been in that much pain before. True to his tough guy-ness, he refused to take an ambulance and insisted on being driven to the hospital.

You see, this man's pain had a very important purpose. If his injury had been manageable, I can assure you he would have come home and iced it for a few days before ever considering seeing a physician. Who knows what kind of damage could have been done if he had waited to see a doctor.

Pain always has a purpose. It sends a message that we need to pay particular attention to something. It insists we acknowledge it and then deal with it. If we ignore it, chances are the injury will fester, resulting in more intense pain. It's a cycle that just spirals us out of control to places we don't want to go.

Ignoring the pain is not worth the gain.

I certainly sought comfort in some very harmful ways. Food was my primary source of comfort. I gained almost 40 pounds in 2 years while I suffered from a broken heart.

For a time, I used alcohol to suppress the pain, and it seemed to work for a while. But then one drink became two and two became three. I remember the exact day I thought it was a smart diet decision to skip dinner, just so I could drink more. Thankfully I was quickly reminded of how my mother would go on an alcohol diet in order to maintain her weight. That was the wake up call I needed.

I remember thinking, "this is becoming a problem. I'm going to have to put a stop to this right away or it will become a vice." That day I did stop, but I am confident that I could have just as easily gone down the familiar path of alcoholism that seemed to plague our family.

Yet not all my comfort came from harmful sources. I also sought comfort in ways that were helpful. Things such as self-help books, counseling, bible study and prayer were all part of my comfort repertoire.

There is hope, even if you've sought the comfort of things not good for you. The purpose of this chapter is to educate you about the healthiest choices for comfort care. Let's discover true comfort that lasts.

I want to share five primary sources of healthy comfort. These 5 things won't come back to bite you. They won't make you gain weight, and they won't become something that you need therapy or recovery for later down the road.

My hope is that as we discover together these five sources of comfort, you would find yourself bathed in the warmth of some much needed compassion and love!

Please note: This is by no means an exhaustive list. These are the five primary ways I've received comfort in my time of need.

Comfort source #1: **Your higher power**—(comfort from a supernatural source)

Higher power is defined as: a spirit or being (such as God) that has great power, strength, knowledge, etc., and that can affect nature and the lives of people.

Our higher power is our number one source of comfort because it's bigger than us. Whether you believe in a creator God, or the universe, or Buddah or something else, it's important to understand and acknowledge that there is something out there greater than us. Leaning into something with more strength, knowledge and wisdom, can be a wonderful source of comfort for our broken heart.

Your higher power understands your need for comfort, better than you do. Therefore, your higher power knows how to comfort you best. Our job becomes allowing our higher power to comfort us.

It's important to remember that while your HP (higher power) desires to comfort you, He will never impose his supernatural comfort upon you. It is a gift that is offered, yet we must (1) ask for it and (2) receive it. It's a free will thing.

Call on your HP today, He'll pick up. He has caller ID and he's expecting your call. Do you ever get frustrated because you can't get hold of someone you need to talk to? Not so with your HP. You'll never get a busy signal, and there's no voice mail saying, "leave a message and I'll call you back."

Connecting to your higher power through prayer or meditation will help you to experience a peace that is greater than understanding...it's supernatural.

For many (myself included), that higher power is our heavenly father—the God of creation. He knows every single detail about each of us, from the number of hairs on our head, to our every thought. He is familiar with all our ways. Every quirk, every idiosyncrasy, every indiscretion, every deep dark secret...He knows them all.

Think about it, how many people in this world would still like you if they knew all those things about you? Probably not many. Yet not only does my higher power know me better than anyone else, He loves me better than anyone else. (I know that was bad English, but I like the way it sounds so I'm sticking with it)

We have been created with a need for comfort and compassion. I believe that same creator also created compassion. I just love knowing that.

When our higher power creates us with a need, He always designs a way to meet that need.

Wouldn't it be great if that was all there was to it? Lean into your higher power and you'll get the comfort you need? Simple as that.

The world offers many unhealthy ways to meet our need for compassion and comfort that are more speedy and instant…a quick fix. We live in a society that is all about finding comfort in the quickest way possible…fast food, quick buck, speed date, high speed internet, etc. The faster the better, right?

Sadly, when it comes to finding healthy comfort for our heart wounds, faster is rarely better. These types of wounds need to heal slowly, from the inside out.

Comfort source #2: **Shared humanity**—(our comfort through connection)

When we recognize that suffering is part of our shared human experience, we can begin the process of understanding that my pain is experienced in many ways, the same as for others. While the situation and degree may vary, the basic experience is the same.

Often this realization can be in direct opposition to our nature that wants to isolate and disconnect from the world around us. Self-pity is in many ways the antithesis to recognizing our shared humanity when it comes to suffering.

Finding Comfort

When a crisis happens and we choose to respond rationally rather than emotionally, it helps us to recognize several important things:

1. We all experience hardships on a regular basis.

This is a universal truth! While our circumstance may feel unique, unfair and unwarranted, in truth, hardship is a part of life, and we will experience many bouts of it throughout our lives.

2. We are not alone in our suffering.

While suffering wants to isolate us from the world, the worst thing we can do is allow our nature to take over and place us in a prison of seclusion. When we recognize that there is nothing new under the sun when it comes to suffering, it allows us to be more understanding and less judgmental toward ourselves and others.

3. Others have gone through this before and more will go through this after.

When we look at our experience with a less personal lens, it can help us to see things from a different perspective.

Now I want to be clear here—this is not about denial. Denial is never healthy. This is about detaching from the personal side of pain, without withdrawing from the experience of betrayal. When we do this, it allows us to recognize the human condition of painful circumstances and encourages us to reach out to seek wisdom, guidance and counsel from those who have gone before us.

Understanding that suffering is shared with all humanity allows us to connect with others and find hope and strength through our common experiences.

> *"Just knowing you are not alone is often enough to kindle hope amid tragic circumstances"*—Richelle E. Goodrich.

That brings us to comfort source #3: **Wise counsel** (comfort from insightful humans)

Wise counsel is closely linked to shared humanity. While shared humanity looks at the whole, wise counsel comes from those who have gone before us.

One of my favorite places to visit is Puerto Penasco on the Sea of Cortez in Mexico. It's only a 4 ½ hour drive from my home and it has become an annual event to go there for my birthday every May. We always stay in an RV park, just steps from the beach. It's breathtakingly beautiful!

Many years ago, for my 41st birthday, I was given one of the most treasured gifts ever while vacationing at that beach in Mexico. It came in the form of a new friendship. I met a beautiful 82-year-old woman when we just happenstance, started talking (I'm an introvert so that rarely happens).

Her name was Eva. We spent most of the day visiting. We talked about children, marriage, life, faith, hardships, betrayal and loss. She shared that she had suddenly lost her first husband at the age of 54 and how she thought her life was over when he passed. Years later, a new man came into her life, and he is now her loving husband, Ray. She talked about her adult children and the struggles in those relationships.

By the end of the day we had shared with one another our deepest hurts as well as our greatest joys. We were hard and fast friends. That night my husband and I treated she and Ray to dinner, and the next day we exchanged contact information and hugs.

Then just like that, she exited my life almost as quickly as she entered it. I believe the universe orchestrated our meeting that day.

This magical unicorn of a woman seemed to be more than familiar with all my ways. Why? Well because she had been down most of my life roads already. She spoke with the voice of experience that showed me a perspective that one only acquires from years of trial and error.

Her wise counsel reached deep into my soul and her sage experience gave me great comfort. That day she was a guiding light, a teacher, and a mentor.

We are blessed to have many avenues in which we can find wise counsel. From therapy to support groups to life mentors to self-help books and more. Finding wise counsel is the easy part, but receiving it requires a few necessary things:

a. Authenticity—we must be willing to be open with others about our hurts. It can seem risky, but it is essential to receiving wise counsel from others.

b. Humility—in order to receive any counsel, we must first acknowledge that we need counsel. Being humble doesn't mean we are less in any way. In fact, it simply means that we are open and willing to hear the insight and perspective of another. Humility is a prerequisite to being teachable.

c. Teachability—"when we think we have things already figured out, we're not teachable. Genuine insight can't

> dawn on a mind that's not open to receive it."—Marianne Williamson, *Return to Love*

When I am in a life crisis, the first thing I do is seek wise counsel. It is a muscle I have strengthened. Oftentimes I seek counsel in many forms—all at once.

I regularly receive clinical counsel from a licensed professional counselor, and I have several women who mentor me in my everyday life. Wise counsel has become a touchstone in my life.

Wise counsel will inject comfort into your weary soul.

Comfort source #4: **Creation** (comfort through diverse experience)

Finding comfort through experiences is something I neglected for many years of my life. Being a mother of four, I was accustomed to neglecting my need to both experience the beauty of creation and to express my own creativity.

Not everyone enjoys creation or nature in the same way. Some are obsessed with it and make it a priority to get outside daily for walks or hikes. Others enjoy watching the sunrise or sunset, while sipping on a cocktail.

A study printed in the April 4, 2019, Frontiers in Psychology, found that spending as little as 20 minutes connecting with nature can help lower stress hormone levels.

Levels of cortisol, a stress hormone, were measured from saliva samples taken before and after nature outings. The people also were instructed to not exercise beforehand and to avoid unrelated stimuli such as social media, phone calls, conversations, and reading. Spending at least 20 to 30 minutes immersed in a nature setting was associated with the biggest drop in cortisol levels.

> *"Nature is my manifestation of God."*—Frank Lloyd Wright

> *"Look deep into nature and then you will understand everything better."*—Albert Einstein

Less cortisol = lower stress = self-comfort and compassion! Talk about a win-win!

Now let's talk about the other side of creation, the action side of creating. To be creative.

Creative: *relating to or involving the imagination or original ideas, especially in the production of an artistic work.*

Discovering ways to have a creative outlet can help you feel more centered and calm.

Again, I struggled with this for many years. The challenge was twofold—finding the time to be creative (raising 4 kids, yo!) and knowing what it was I enjoyed creating. Sometimes it takes a bit of trial and error to know what it is you enjoy creating. I've tried crafts, scrapbooking, music lessons, crochet, baking, dancing and more. But at the end of the day the two things I enjoy creating the most are writing and home renovation projects.

I encourage you to find your creative outlet and spend time with it. It in turn will get your mind off of your circumstances while filling your heart with some much needed self-compassion and comfort.

And finally, comfort source #5: **Friends** (comfort from emotional support)

We all need emotional support when we are hurting, and a good friend will meet that need. We all know the qualities of a good friend: loyal, honest, dependable, supportive, a good listener, an encourager.

There is nothing like that soul-level friend who can lift you up when you're down, bring you down when your head's stuck in the clouds and just sit with you when you're sad. We all need this sort of friend!

But I want you to notice that I've listed 'friends' last. I've done this intentionally and for a reason.

Now I want you to take a moment and indulge me, as we look at these five sources of comfort from a statistical standpoint. There is a point I'm trying to make here, other than that math is hard.

If you put those five sources of comfort into a statistical equation, together they would equal 100% of the comfort you need to receive when life's got you down.

- Higher Power = 20%
- Shared Humanity = 20%
- Wise Counsel = 20%
- Creation = 20%
- Friends = 20%

Now for just a moment I want you to think about those five sources of comfort. Four of those five come to us in ways that are higher or bigger than us. Meaning they are ways to find comfort that we can only find through higher level thinking or inspiration.

The comfort we get from friends is the only comfort that does not require an enlightened mind. Enlightened: *having or showing a rational, modern and well-informed outlook.*

Statistically, that means 80% of our comfort should come from a source of enlightenment, or something bigger than us, while 20% of our comfort should come from friends and loved ones.

This is by design and of great importance.

Yet what most of us do is we flip-flop those numbers. Our nature is to seek 80% of our comfort from our friends and only 20% from an enlightened mind.

Is it any wonder we often feel our need for comfort goes unmet?

You see, the universe wants to comfort you in many ways. My hope for you is that you will decide to actively and intentionally seek comfort from those enlightened sources first and only then reach out to your friends.

One important point I want to make here is that the healthiest types of comfort aren't always immediate. We may even give up seeking comfort because we don't feel comforted in the way we WANT, when we want it.

It's the old adage; 'I want what I want, when I want it!' So when we don't get immediate satisfaction, we give up. That's when things like alcohol, drugs, food and shopping become so appealing to us...the payoff is instantaneous.

Yet I assure you, worldly comforts do not come close to comparing to the kind of comfort an enlightened mind can give you. Decide today that you are going to be intentional about receiving comfort from all 5 sources—I assure you, you won't regret it!

Chapter 6
What happens to wounds that are not properly comforted

I have some good news and some bad news to start this chapter. The good news is that you have come this far! I've thrown quite a lot at you. By now you should have a clear understanding of the importance of connecting with others who have been where you are. By this point you should grasp how important finding healthy comfort is for your heart wounds. And you now have many resources for finding healthy comfort for your broken heart.

Now for the bad news...

Here comes the hard stuff. Starting now, we'll begin to look at the damage that happens to us when we stay stuck in our brokenheartedness for too long.

Trust me, it's not pretty. I should know. I spent several years stuck in bitterness, and it wreaked all kinds of havoc in my life.

Just being given resources to care for our crushed heart and spirit isn't enough. Eventually we must take the next step towards acceptance and ultimately forgiveness. For no other reason other than acceptance and forgiveness is what's best for us.

You've probably heard the analogy that holding onto hurts is like drinking poison, in the hope that it will harm the person who hurt you. It ends up hurting us more than anyone else.

So, what is that next step? Well simple really...simple yet not easy.

Letting go of the hurt

Acceptance and forgiveness take time. Sometimes a long time and only you (with the help of your enlightened mind) can determine exactly how much time it takes for you to let go and forgive the hurts in your life. There is no scale or formula for how much time it should take, yet there are some distinct signs that will let you know when you've held onto a hurt for too long. Let's take a look at what happens when we're unwilling to let go of and forgive the hurt.

Holding onto our hurts and clinging to our brokenheartedness for too long will cause some detrimental things to begin to manifest in our lives.

What happens to a physical wound if it's ignored for too long or closed off from the environment? It becomes infected. That same principle is true when it comes to heart wounds.

Uncared-for heart wounds will become infected

Relational or emotional wounds are in many ways similar to a physical wound. A wound from a betrayal or loss, if not properly cared for can become a scabbed over, infected gash that festers and oozes. Like I said earlier, it's not pretty.

Remember the story I shared a few chapters back, about my injured foot at the beach? Imagine what could have happened if I chose not to have it cleaned out and stitched up. What if I had decided that I was just going to wait and see if it healed on its own? There's a good chance it would have become infected with all that sand and other oceany things that could have gotten into that wound. Eventually the pain would have increased over time, until I could no longer endure it. Who knows what might have happened. I'm confident that getting it cared for that day was the best choice.

In contrast, when it came to emotional and relational hurts, I certainly chose a very different path. I didn't jump in the car and drive to heartbreak hospital...nope. I chose to ignore it until it festered and became a very dark and ugly wound that took several years to finally heal.

I held onto my hurts for so long that eventually my heart became infected with bitterness.

Bitterness is an iniquity

Iniquity*: immoral or grossly unfair behavior.*

It's this infection of bitterness that makes heartbreak such a tricky thing. You see, wounds never stay in their injured state. They either heal over time (the amount of time varies...we'll talk about that in a later chapter), or they will become infected.

Infected heart wounds manifest into disappointment, anger, resentment and bitterness. Our hearts either slowly heal or they will slowly get infected.

The simple truth is that...

What happens to wounds that are not properly comforted

"We **must** rehabilitate or **we will** relapse."

Rehabilitate: *restore (someone) to health or normal life by training and therapy after imprisonment, addiction, or illness.*

Relapse: *a deterioration in someone's state of health after a temporary improvement.*

There are only two directions we can go in our journey toward letting go of our hurts. Either we move in the direction of rehabilitation, or we move in the direction of relapse. If we don't pursue health and healing we will become more ill. There is no middle/neutral ground.

While brokenheartedness is not an inequity. Having an unforgiving spirit, harboring bitterness and resentment IS.

Now let's look at three key words in this chapter: unforgiveness, resentment, and bitterness.

Definition of **forgiveness**: *To cease to blame or to cease to feel resentment against.*

The prefix 'un' means 'the inability to'. Therefore, another way to look at that word unforgiveness is as:

the inability to cease to blame or feel resentment against.

Synonyms of **forgiveness**: *mercy, pardon, exonerate.*

Hence, **unforgiveness** defined is: *the inability to do the above three things. Show mercy, pardon or exonerate.*

Definition of **resentment**: *Aggrieved feelings caused by a sense of having been badly treated.*

Synonyms of **resentment**: anger, bitterness, dislike, hatred

Definition of **bitterness**: *Being characterized by intense antagonism or hostility— resentful or cynical*

Synonyms of **bitterness**: sour, angry, harsh, intense spitefulness.

Okay, listen because this is important. Brokenheartedness is an inward focused hurt. It's characterized by looking at and examining oneself. Focusing on your wound and your heart. Our feelings are primarily inward focused, and we say and think things like: 'I'm hurting', 'I'm struggling', 'my heart is broken', 'I can't believe this is happening'.

In contrast, unforgiveness, resentment and bitterness are all outward focused. They are more characterized by looking at or examining what others have done to us. Our focus is no longer on our own wounds but is now on the actions of others. We say and think things that are more outward focused like: 'He betrayed me', 'She broke my heart', 'can you believe they did this?'

Now I'm aware this is not an exact science or a perfect analogy, but it is an important thing to think about and consider. If we listen close enough our hearts will tell us if we've transitioned from hurt to bitter.

Brokenheartedness is more focused on our own wounds with a desire to find relief or comfort from the pain caused by those wounds.

Unforgiveness, resentment and bitterness change our focus from our own personal pain to another person's action that caused that pain.

It's the difference between looking in a mirror at your own reflection, and looking at someone else with a magnifying glass.

What happens to wounds that are not properly comforted

It's time we put down our magnifying glass and pick up our make-up mirror. You know the one I'm talking about. It's a 2-sided, lighted mirror that magnifies on one side. (I've actually never owned one in real life. I do NOT want to see this face magnified!)

It's time to take a really close, magnified look at your heart. (remember I told you this would be hard work!) Don't just glance at it but really study it. What do you see?

Are you:

- Antagonistic (unfriendly, expressing opposition)
- Hostile (showing or feeling hatred or anger toward somebody)
- Resentful (annoyed, angry)
- Cynical (negative, distrustful of human nature)
- Aggrieved (having a desire to cause distress, pain or trouble to another)
- Any negative feelings I might have left out?

Oftentimes, we aren't able to recognize these negative behaviors in our own lives.

Now might be a good time to consider reaching out to someone who knows you, and who you trust to speak the truth. Ask them if they see any of these characteristics in you, but only if you can handle hearing what they might say. Make sure it is someone safe, who truly has your best interest at heart. You're not looking for criticism, you're looking for an honest observation.

I wasn't at all able to recognize that I had become so outwardly focused on my hurt. I was all those negative things I listed above (hostile, cynical, antagonistic, etc.), I just didn't see it. Those who knew me best sure could see it. Sadly, my family had a front row seat to my bitter behaviors.

Please remember the goal here in reaching out to a trusted friend, is NOT to end up even more hurt. Going to a friend requires really being willing to hear whatever they share. You may (or may not) be surprised.

Don't allow yourself to get defensive when your trusted friend tells you something you don't want to hear. Remember, this person wants what's best for you and they would never say something just to hurt you. Oftentimes, when I am told something that seems harsh or hurts my feelings, I give myself a full day (24 hours) to process it. Generally, after that amount of time I'm able to see it in a more reasonable manner.

Another important thing to keep in mind is that all of those negative behavioral words I've listed above have the appearance of aggressive, assertive, out-going, harsh behavior. But let me assure you, every single one of them can be (and often is) displayed with passivity.

I'm a "B" personality...an introvert. I am reserved and quiet yet in my passive way I've exhibited **every one** of those unattractive behaviors. Hopefully not all at once. Rarely to friends and NEVER to acquaintances or strangers because that would just be rude.

I saved most (if not all) of my ugly behavior for those closest and dearest to me. Namely, my husband. I really put him through hell. Unfortunately, my children have also been on the receiving end of much of my passive aggressive bitter behaviors.

Our hearts will try to convince us to hold onto our hurts, rationalizing that clinging to them will in turn protect us from further hurt. While that may sound like a good idea, it isn't.

Believing that we should hold onto our hurts is nothing more than a convincing lie. It has the appearance of reason, so we believe it. Building a fortress around our heart in an effort to protect it from further injury makes perfect sense, right? In truth, cutting our heart off from hurt only ends up doing more damage to us than we ever thought possible.

Years ago, my son thought it would be fun to slide down the banister of our stairs. Needless to say, he fell and broke his arm. He had a cast that extended past his elbow for the typical eight weeks. This cast kept his arm in a bent position while the bone healed.

Strangely, once they removed the cast, his arm didn't straighten out. Months later I took him back to the doctor to get it checked out. The doctor twisted and bent the arm and then told me that the inability to straighten his arm was all in my son's cute little nine-year-old head. His arm was totally healed, only he didn't believe it. It stayed bent because he was protecting it from getting injured again.

It took time, physical therapy and then more time to finally convince this boy that it was okay to straighten his arm.

That's what we do with our heart wounds. We convince ourselves that we are still injured and that we still need comfort. Even though the universe is nudging us to move forward and encouraging us to let go of our hurt so that we can be healthy and healed, we are too afraid. We refuse to believe our wound has been healed and we refuse to trust that it's okay to move on.

It took me a long, long time to finally believe I was no longer brokenhearted. By the time I realized it, I was neck-deep and full of the infection of unforgiveness, resentment and bitterness.

I'm sorry to say you are most likely on the path towards bitterness as well. Or maybe like me, you've arrived at your final destination, the pit of bitterness, and you've taken up residence there. Chances are you're stuck in the mire. I can relate; I've been there.

Mire: *a situation or state of difficulty, distress, or embarrassment from which it is hard to extricate oneself. He has been left to squirm in a mire of new allegations.*

Decades ago, I was asked to teach a lesson on 'forgiveness'. I started my teaching with what I knew best...'unforgiveness'. In preparation, of course I researched the topic of unforgiveness and for some reason I kept coming across the word—'bitterness'.

To be honest, I was quite put off by this word. It seemed so abrasive and caustic. I preferred thinking of myself as, 'having an unforgiving spirit'. For some reason the word 'bitterness' left a (for lack of a better word) bitter taste in my mouth. It sounded too harsh, too severe.

I believe that day I was being shown that unforgiveness, resentment and bitterness all go hand in hand. If you have an unforgiving spirit, over time it will turn into resentment. That resentment over time will become bitterness. It's a natural progression.

We must do something completely against our nature in order to put a stop to that natural progression of bitterness from developing in our lives.

When I taught that first lesson on forgiveness, decades ago, I never once used the word 'bitterness'. I wasn't ready to admit to myself that I was in fact...bitter.

That's what some would call 'being in denial'. I spent so much time in the waters of denial, my fingers got all wrinkly.

Now let's do something really fun...let's explore anger. Aren't you excited!? Sorry for the sarcasm here—I just felt we needed a little lightheartedness to lighten the mood.

Anger is one of the primary emotions produced when harboring unforgiveness, resentment and bitterness.

If you look up the word 'anger' in a thesaurus there is actually a surprising range of synonyms for anger—everything from 'annoyance' and 'irritation' to 'infuriate' and 'rage.'

Anger covers a **wide** variety of emotions. It's not just wild eyed, crazy, out of control rage, it's also being aggravated, exasperated, frustrated, impatient and cross. All are forms of anger.

When is anger wrong?

> *"As a natural human emotion, anger is neither right nor wrong in itself. It can be used for either good or evil-just as a knife can be a surgeon's scalpel or a murderer's weapon. Anger can be a powerful tool for confronting wrong. Selfish or manipulative anger, however, can cause great harm. Such anger becomes destructive when it controls us rather than us controlling it."*—Quest Study Bible

When is anger okay?

> *"Anger is a God-given human emotion and not sinful in*

> *itself...In fact, anger at sin, injustice and evil is a sign of godliness and righteousness. But anger that leads to malice, rage and revenge is clearly forbidden and should be handled quickly to prevent damaging attitudes and actions."*—
> Quest Study Bible

Anger in and of itself is a natural human emotion. As a human emotion it is morally neutral, neither good nor bad. It's what we do with our anger that determines whether or not we are in the wrong.

In my opinion, there are very few times when our anger is absolutely 100% righteous. I believe that even if we start out with the right kind of anger, we must monitor it closely to be sure that our anger does not become malicious. Most anger is the kind that leads to damaging attitudes and actions.

Anger usually controls us and is destructive, and managing it is like walking a tightrope. It requires a lot of concentration, balance and control. Anger and control usually are not seen together. In fact, destructive anger is usually expressed due to a lack of control.

Now don't get me wrong, every single person who has been hurt absolutely should feel some sort of anger! It's normal and right to be angry at the person who betrayed you. Anger at your higher power or the universe for the loss of a loved one is understandable, and anger at ourselves for the hurtful things we've done is to be expected.

When we've received a heart wound, it puts us on a grieving path, and one of the steps in that process is anger. You are probably familiar with the five steps of grieving but let's share them with you anyway.

What happens to wounds that are not properly comforted

They are:

1. **Denial** (to declare that something is not true)
2. **Anger** (a strong feeling of grievance and displeasure)
3. **Bargaining** (to negotiate the terms—exchange one thing for another)
4. **Depression** (a state of unhappiness and hopelessness)
5. **Acceptance** (willingness to believe, tolerance)

Anger is one of the steps we **all** take on our paths to acceptance and peace. But we must be vigilant with our anger so that it does not become sin. To completely avoid the step of anger is unhealthy and will inhibit our healing process.

Right after my heartbreak, I spent a few years avoiding anger. I'd jump all around it, but I would never allow myself to really get angry. Sure, it leaked out in unexpected and passive ways, because it had to.

Mostly my anger seeped out onto my kids and husband. I'd wake up in a bad mood and be edgy the entire day for no apparent reason. Something would remind me that I didn't deserve to be hurt, and it wasn't fair. I'd spend the day being annoyed at anyone in my atmosphere.

I remember a time when my oldest child asked me why I was yelling at the dog. I replied, "Because I'm in a bad mood!" "Well, why?" my son asked. "I honestly have no idea. I just am." I responded.

We can't skip any of the steps in the grieving process. By the time I allowed myself to get angry, boy did it slam into my life like a ton of bricks. I was mad! Mad at the person who hurt me, mad at my higher power, mad at myself for letting this happen, mad at the world, even mad at the dog.

Healthy anger needs strict boundaries and parameters and constant supervision. Even if we get it right and our anger is the righteous kind, we must deal with that righteous anger quickly. Ideally—THAT SAME DAY. It's best to deal with all anger quickly. As impossible as that may seem, it is for our protection, our own good, so that it doesn't become the wrong kind of anger.

You see, if we let anger linger for too long, we give it a foothold in our heart and mind. Want to know what a foothold is?

"A secure starting position from which further advances can be made."

That's what WE GIVE our anger if we hold onto it for too long. Why would we willingly give something so destructive as anger a secure position in our lives where advances in anger can be made? Anger in and of itself *does not* have the power to take a foothold in our lives; we give it a foothold by holding onto anger for too long.

It's like we're saying:

> *"Here you go, destructive anger. I'm not ready to let go of you just yet, so here's my gift to you. A nice little place in my life where you can start to wreak havoc. Isn't that great!? I'll even wrap it in pink paper and put a big bow on top for you. Enjoy!"*

I convinced myself that holding onto my anger was the right thing to do. I would rationalize my choice by thinking, "I'm justified in my anger. After all, look at what was done to me in order for me to be this angry."

I thought my brokenheartedness warranted my anger. Turns out, all it did was give anger a secure little spot in my life where it could plan to make advancements.

What are anger's advancements you ask? Good question (dang you're smart!) In our next chapter we are going to dive into that fun subject. But for now, I'm going to share part of a very real, very raw entry from my personal journal, just to give you a glimpse of what was going on in my head when I was trapped in resentment.

> 9/12/06
> *God,*
> *I'm in need of an intervention now. I'm feeling very lonely and brokenhearted. I'm where I knew I'd be...stuck...still stuck! How long am I going to be stuck like this? I want to move forward, I just don't know how to. I truly desire healing, yet whenever I look at my situation I am instantly discouraged and completely hopeless. Lately it seems that all my efforts don't make any difference and I'm sick of trying so hard!*
> *The moment I feel like I'm starting to recover from my broken heart, something hurtful happens and it rips the scab right off. I* JUST WANT OUT OF THIS PAINFUL FIRE!
> *I am comforted by knowing that eventually the pain will lessen, but I am weary in the waiting. Please help me get out of this furnace of suffering!*

If you feel like you are in a furnace of suffering, please hang on.

There is purpose in the pain if you allow it to mold you into something stronger.

> *"Suffering has been stronger than all other teaching, and has taught me to understand what your heart used to be. I have been bent and broken, but - I hope - into a better shape."*—Charles Dickens**,** *Great Expectations*

> *"Out of suffering have emerged the strongest souls; the most massive characters are seared with scars."*—Kahlil Gibran

> *"See, I have refined you, though not as silver; I have tested you in the furnace of affliction."*—Isaiah 48:10

Refine: *to remove impurities or unwanted elements from a substance.*

Synonyms of **refine**: *purify, process, improve, perfect, enhance, sharpen, make better.*

If we allow it, suffering can be a process of improving and strengthening us.

I believe suffering is one of the most effective ways we can be refined in life. Not that anyone would want to experience suffering, however, as we know, it is not optional. We will all suffer at some point in our lives.

Many people believe that the cycle of life revolves around moments of crisis in our lives, and we are in one of 3 places in our lives:

1. Moving toward a life crisis.
2. Currently in a life crisis.
3. Moving out of a life crisis.

This life perspective teaches that our lives will all be marked by moments of intense difficulty or trouble. While I'm not a huge fan of this life perspective, I do believe it has validity. When I look back at my life, I can see the pockmarks where a crisis hit. Truthfully, every one of those moments became a life lesson.

When we begin to understand that suffering is part of life, it can change how we see life, giving us the ability to expect crisis and hardship, encouraging us to find the golden nugget of wisdom that hurts can teach us.

Waking up every day with the understanding that life will have hard times, has taught me to appreciate the good days even more and not be surprised when the unexpected sucker-punches me right in the gut.

My hope for you is that you are able to recognize where you are in your heartbreak. That you will be able to acknowledge if you've held onto your hurts for too long and if you have become bitter. And finally, that you keep working through letting go of your hurts, so that you can truly heal.

Chapter 7
Consequences of bitterness
Part 1

Once we hold onto anger for too long, we will begin to experience the ugly consequences of unforgiveness. It can be in many forms: disappointment, resentment, bitterness. The byproduct of unforgiveness can be very serious and quite harmful, damaging us relationally, spiritually, emotionally and physically.

Something must be done to get us out of bitterness!

Something to note is that oftentimes, the consequences of bitterness are invisible and silent. They can go undetected for long periods of time because we are either completely unaware of their presence, or we're ignorant of their potential for destruction in our lives.

Almost like an undiagnosed cancer, if left untreated it can have fatal results. Bitterness is a cancer so silent that it can be difficult to diagnose. Thankfully, once bitterness is identified it can be treated, and the good news is that this cancer, once treated, has a 100% survival rate.

Cancer: *a fast-spreading bad phenomenon. Something negative that develops or spreads quickly and usually destructively.*

This chapter's objective is to help you identify and diagnose your condition. With the experience and wise words of those who have gone before us, together we can come up with a treatment regimen —understanding that the ultimate goal is to reestablish health, body, mind and soul.

The world may do its best to convince you that you don't have this cancer of bitterness. I wanted to believe that I didn't need treatment because I wasn't sick. I thought I had every reasonable right to be angry and by the time I figured out that I had this 'fast-spreading bad phenomenon', it had already caused significant destruction in my life.

Common sense tells us that when someone betrays us, we should no longer trust them, plain and simple. Health speaks a different language and actually wants us to let go of the VERY things we believe we have a right to hold on to: anger, revenge, discouragement, depression, disappointment. It may not make sense to us, and it may not seem fair to us. But it is what is best for us!

Let's explore the four basic consequences of bitterness.

1 Bitterness can affect our personality & character - causing us to change our outlook on life.

- From positive to critical/negative.
- From calm/patient to angry/edgy.
- From being kind/generous to sarcastic/selfish.
- From happy/joyful to sad/miserable.

I used to say I wish people knew me BEFORE my heart was wounded because my personality changed once I was mired down in bitterness. I was fun-loving and happy before and characterized by being negative and sad after. It felt like a dark storm-cloud followed me around all the time. I could relate to Eeyore from *Winnie the Pooh*.

> **"It's snowing still," said Eeyore gloomily.**
> **"So it is."**
> **"And freezing." "Is it?"**
> **"Yes," said Eeyore. "However," he said, brightening up a little, "we haven't had an earthquake lately."**

That was me. Even my happy moments were overshadowed by gloominess. Woe was me. Or is it...woe was I? Oh, who cares—just woe everything.

Growing up in my family, when we'd catch someone feeling sorry for themselves, we would try and lift their spirits with an old Hee-Haw song...

Gloom, despair, and agony on me
Deep, dark depression,
excessive misery: If it weren't for bad luck, I'd have no luck at all
Gloom, despair, and agony on me

Believe it or not, that song usually lightens the mood. Try singing it sometime. It's hilarious.

Sometimes a lighthearted moment is exactly what the doctor ordered. But right now, it's time to get serious again...

Consequences of bitterness Part 1

"My friends and companions avoid me because of my wounds; my neighbors stay far away."—Psalm 38:11

I could have written that verse as it described me to a tee. People understandably avoided me when I was wounded. At the time, I saw it through my own negative, critical eyes. I criticized my church for abandoning me. I questioned many of my friendships because the distance grew between us. The only thing keeping my few girlfriends around was loyalty. They'd call every week or two just to check in, knowing they would be on the receiving end of an earful of my indignation.

I didn't understand it at all. A few years before when my grandmother (who was like a mother to me) passed away, I had friends coming out of the woodwork to care for and comfort me. They offered food, childcare, food, housecleaning, oh and did I mention food? Several of them even came to the funeral on the other side of town just to be there for me. They even put together a care basket with snacks, a prayer book and little trinkets. The show of kindness and support was overwhelming.

Yet in contrast...

When my marriage fell apart, one friend sent a note saying she was praying for me. Other than that, there was no rallying of the comfort brigade. There were no baskets with treats and little prayer books. No house cleaning or meals. Just a lot of awkwardness, advice and avoidance.

Eventually the question I had to ask myself was "what changed?" Why did so many surround me in love and care when my grandmother passed, yet no one was around when my marriage fell apart?

My church hadn't changed; my friends were the same. The only other option was...it must have been me. I was the common denominator. I changed. Today I can look back and say...

"I wouldn't have wanted to be friends with me."

For many in my friend group, the whole situation was awkward and uncomfortable. It was easy to comfort me when my loved one passed, but what do you say or do in a situation like the one I was in now?

Within a few years, many of my friends started avoiding me because of my wounds. I was no longer getting invited to lunch or play dates at the park.

Now I see why. After all, who in their right mind would want to hang around and watch my heart wound fester and ooze with bitterness? It became more than my friends could stand. I was not good company.

I see now that it was me. That I had changed.

Yet there was still hope for me. Even after spending five long years in the pit of bitterness, I still found a way out, and so can you! What I know for sure is that you can reverse the effects of unforgiveness, disappointment, resentment and bitterness. Maybe not overnight, but slowly and steadily as you learn to let go of your hurts. We CAN re-train ourselves to react differently when a life crisis hits. We'll discuss that more in a later chapter.

Now let's look at the second consequence of bitterness:

2 Bitterness affects our relationships.

One thing I know for sure, nobody wants to be around someone who is bitter or unforgiving. It's draining to be in the company of someone who is negative, critical, sad, harsh and so on.

Unforgiveness has affected every important relationship in my life. From my friends (we already talked about that) to my kids. Of course, my relationship with my husband was greatly affected by my bitterness. It even affected a relationship that was unexpected...more on that in a bit.

Believe it or not, it was primarily my own bitterness that kept my children in limbo for almost five years, never knowing if mom and dad were going to stay married or get divorced.

My number one priority in life has always been my kids. I'd tell my husband that if ever there was a fire in our home, he was on his own because I'm saving the kids! I was passionately committed to raising them with a love for family and for the world around us. My number one goal in parenting has been to instill in them strength of character. So when I realized that it was actually MY inability to forgive that was the primary reason my children were so insecure about our family, my heart was absolutely crushed!

Here I was teaching my kids to forgive yet I wasn't able to practice what I was preaching. Inadvertently, I was doing the same thing to my children that my father did to me. 'Do as I say, not as I do' my father would always say.

I deeply regret holding onto my resentments for so long because I see how it affected my children. For years, whenever their dad went on a business trip they would ask, 'Is daddy coming home?' It broke my heart every time they would ask that question, and it even makes me tear up today.

I would never intentionally try to hurt my kids, but my bitterness certainly did a number on their sense of security!

It goes without saying that every aspect of my marriage relationship was affected by my bitterness. Intimacy, trust, security, friendship, you name it...all very damaged. My husband diligently worked on his recovery and committed himself to becoming the very best father and husband he could be. It had become my behavior in this relationship that was unhealthy. I was the one pushing him away because I couldn't let go of the hurt. I couldn't forgive. I couldn't move on. I constantly reminded my husband what a bad person he was because of the things he did. I was relentless. My mind couldn't grasp how he could have done those things, and I didn't think it was possible to **EVER** trust him with my heart again.

The tables had turned, and I was now the one damaging this primary relationship.

"Harping should be limited to musical instruments."— Charmaine Smith Ladd

"A worthy wife is her husband's joy and crown; the other kind corrodes his strength and tears down everything he does. "—Proverbs 12:4 (TLB)

Unbeknownst to me, I had become a harping, 'the other kind' of wife.

How about you, would you consider yourself a 'worthy' spouse, or 'the other kind'? Have you corroded the strength of those around you?

Maybe it's not your spouse who has hurt you. Maybe it's a friend or family member who has betrayed your trust. If your bitterness is not in regard to your marriage, those last few sentences probably don't speak to you. Regardless of who is the subject of your bitterness, if you are harboring any unforgiveness in your heart, then it has affected your primary relationships in some way. Maybe you don't trust, or you are closed off. Maybe you're needy or codependent.

I remember thinking that I was the one who got the worst of the person who hurt me (my husband) but now someone else was going to reap the benefits of his changed life. Afterall, he *was* changing into the person I always wanted him to be, but I couldn't figure out how to let go of the hurt so that I could enjoy the benefits.

I knew deep down that this relationship had a chance to survive and even thrive if I could just let go of the bitterness, but I truly didn't know how to. I wanted to. I tried to. I just couldn't.

At one point, about 3 ½ years after my heartbreak injury, I was *desperate* for help, so I sought out yet another 'great counselor.' On my second visit, I tearfully *pleaded* with him, begging him to:

> "Please, help me forgive. I really want to. I do. Please tell
> me how to forgive. I need a step-by-step process.
> HELP ME!"

His exact words to me were...

> ”Well, honestly, you just choose to forgive and then you forgive.”

I sat in his office sobbing uncontrollably. I’m pretty sure he was irritated with me because I had used up an entire box of Kleenex in an effort to sop up all the snot and tears gushing from my face. And since there was no trash can in sight, I just kept balling up the tissues until there was a softball sized wad sitting in my lap. Not one of my most attractive moments. I’m NOT a pretty crier.

Our conversation continued...

> “Okay, I want to forgive, but can you tell me how?” I asked earnestly. “Well, like I said, you just do.” He reiterated.
>
> “I want to...I just don’t know how to...can you tell me what it would look like for me to forgive? Can you give me the steps?” I was desperate.
>
> “You just choose to do it, and then you do it!” was his tiresome reply. “I hear you, I just don’t understand.” I sobbed.
>
> “You know what? I don’t think I’m the right counselor for you.”

With that, I paid the man and left. My lovely departure gift was a box of used tissues molded into the shape of a sphere...very artistic.

I felt like I was in quicksand, desperate to grab onto anything that would pull me out, but just getting myself more and more trapped. I was stuck and sinking fast.

Thankfully I didn't give up hope. I knew there was a way to forgive. I just needed to figure out what the steps were. That is the motivation and reason for my writing this book -- to help those who feel how I was feeling. To help those who want to heal but just don't know how to heal.

There was an unexpected relationship that was affected by my bitterness. It was my relationship with me. I thought I was so many things that I wasn't. The very day my life came crashing down around me I was teaching vacation Bible school at our church. I was confident in my spiritual leadership abilities, probably to the point of arrogance. Then everything fell apart. Soon after, all self-confidence was replaced with an overwhelming sense of self disgust and shame. I quickly decided that I was unqualified to do little more than clean toilets at my church.

In truth, I felt more disqualified than unqualified. One definition of disqualified is, **to declare unfit**. That's what I did. I declared myself unfit to lead or teach anyone. No one told me I was unfit or unqualified. I declared it upon myself.

I was engulfed by self-condemnation and flooded by feelings of **shame.** I knew it wasn't reasonable and didn't make sense, after all, I was the victim. I didn't betray the marriage, but I couldn't let go of the shame. It defined me.

Shame: *A negative emotion that combines feelings of dishonor, unworthiness, and embarrassment.*

That's exactly how I felt, unworthy, embarrassed, dishonored and ashamed.

For over a year all I felt qualified to do in the area of serving at church was to clean. It was something I could do when no one else was around. As the universe would have it, this season of service turned out to be more therapeutic and rewarding than I could have ever imagined.

I believe my higher power used my time of scrubbing toilets and mopping floors to prepare me for something new. He led my husband and I into helping launch a recovery ministry at our church, where others could come to a place of acceptance, safety, encouragement and support. And now God has equipped me to help the brokenhearted heal their wounds. These have been **by far** the most rewarding ministries I have *ever* had the honor of being a part of. I love helping broken people find help and healing.

I see today how my shame and humiliation led to ultimately strengthening my message and preparing me to pursue health and help others do the same. I am grateful. I believe it is only because of the process I've gone through that I am able to help those who are hurting.

Today I can say that my relationship with myself is stronger and healthier than ever!

3 Bitterness affects our bodies.

Our bodies were not created for stress, suffering or trauma. Think about it, if our bodies were created to handle those things, then we would never need to seek comfort. We would have no need for recovery programs because we wouldn't turn to outside things for relief.

Wouldn't it be helpful if our body could simply dispense caffeine, painkillers or a sleep aid when needed? As nice as that would be, I believe our physical bodies were not created that way because the powers that be want us to seek help outside ourselves when we are struggling. And since we have been given free will, we can always seek unhealthy things to meet our need for comfort.

> *"The only way to find yourself is in times of sorrow."*—
> Oswald Chambers

Another way to put it is, *suffering creates substance.*

When suffering is dealt with in a healthy way it can generate an intellectual and emotional complexity in us and in turn, that complexity strengthens us.

Sorrow and pain can be (if we allow it) a catalyst for a spiritual, emotional and relational growth spurt. That's the upside to suffering (if there is one).

But then we also must consider Newton's third law of motion:

> *For every action there is an equal and opposite reaction.*

For every upside there is an equal downside. It's the downside that will destroy us if we allow it.

I have often thought that life would be so much simpler if our higher power would just force us to trust and depend on him or her, rather than giving us a choice. We must choose to trust the process of suffering and believe that in that suffering, we will come out of it stronger than ever!

> *"Character cannot be developed in ease and quiet. Only through experience of trial and suffering can the soul be strengthened, ambition inspired, and success achieved."*–
> Helen Keller

> *"The reward of suffering is experience."*—Harry S. Truman

> *"I do not believe that sheer suffering teaches. If suffering*

> *alone taught, all the world would be wise, since everyone suffers. To suffering must be added mourning, understanding, patience, love, openness and the willingness to remain vulnerable."* - Ann Morrow Lindbergh

Many years ago I struggled with overwhelming physical exhaustion. I never felt I had a good night's sleep. The doctors did bloodwork and ordered a sleep study to be done, all in an effort to determine the cause of my constant state of lethargy. Every test came back 'normal'. The doctor explained that sometimes there are no answers, and I was diagnosed with chronic fatigue syndrome. When I asked what my treatments were, the doctor said, "Nothing really, just keep an eye on it and if anything changes let us know."

A few years after that, I woke up one morning with half my face paralyzed. We rushed to the doctor's office and again, loads of tests. I had a case of Bell's palsy. At the time there was no known treatment. I was told to go home and monitor it and that it could go away in a few days, weeks, months or possibly never. It did go away after several months. My family found it amusing to make me laugh because only half my face would react. Going out in public was embarrassing. Eating was embarrassing and even being in public view was a challenge as others would notice.

I am personally convinced that things kept happening to my body because there was so much going on in my life that needed attention, yet I chose to just ignore it all. I believe the physical symptoms were messages my body was trying to send to my brain that something was wrong and needed attention. My emotional, spiritual and relational life was a complete mess and after a while, my body started sending smoke signals. I was completely unaware that my physical ailments could have been anything other than a physical thing, so when I didn't get any answers from the medical field, I just chose to continue to ignore it.

I have always had a tendency to get sick after a high stress time in my life. I've spent many Christmas days in bed due to overexerting myself in order to make the holiday a magical one. There's a lot of stress that comes along with the holidays. All the running around, all the gifts to buy and wrap. For years we hosted an annual gingerbread house decorating party for over 100 friends in early December. The stress of planning and paying for that party always took a hefty toll on my body. I'd push my body beyond its limits and then it would rebel and shut down.

No matter what form stress comes in, it takes a toll. Being unforgiving, bitter and resentful causes a lot of stress and anxiety in our lives. Stress and anxiety are poison to our bodies. I can guarantee that if you are bitter, you've had your share of physical ailments and ignoring it won't make it go away.

If our emotional well-being affects our physical well-being, then it only stands to reason that emotional pain, when left unchecked and undealt with, will cause some significant physical issues.

> *"A heart at peace gives life to the body, but envy rots the bones."* - Proverbs 14:30

> *"A sound mind makes for a robust body, but runaway emotions corrode the bones."*—Proverbs 14:30 (Message)

If a heart at peace gives life to the body, then we should pursue peace...don't you think?

I hope you can chase after peace and health, for your mind, body and soul.

Today I no longer struggle with fatigue as physically I feel better than I have in years. My joints aren't as sore and stiff, and I have significantly more energy. I believe my physical health has been directly affected by my ability to finally let go of the hurt and figure out how to finally forgive.

Chapter 8
Consequences of bitterness
Part 2

In the last chapter we covered many consequences of bitterness. We learned how it can influence one's personality, character or outlook on life. Then we looked at how unforgiveness affects our relationships. Finally, we ruminated about the damage that holding onto our hurts for too long can do to our bodies.

Now let's take an in-depth look at one more consequence of bitterness. In my opinion this consequence is by far the most damaging.

Bitterness affects our belief system.

Belief system: *a set of principles or tenets which together form the basis of a religion, philosophy, or moral code.*

Right now you may be thinking; "I already know what that means. What is up with this crazy woman and her constantly sharing the definitions of words I already know the meaning of? Jeez-Louise."

I find it helpful to read the definitions of words I already know the meaning of. It helps me to look for new insight from the definition of a word. It may seem excessive or odd but please bear with me.

On my path to figuring out forgiveness, I realized that my belief system was much weaker than I had originally thought. In hindsight, I see that I had an 'if/then' set of beliefs. I believed that *if* I did the right thing, *then* I would be spared from unjust suffering. That type of thinking was a very fragile system of beliefs. While my beliefs had the appearance of strength and wisdom, in truth they could easily be broken and when my life crisis hit, my belief system shattered.

I had some serious entitlement issues that I projected into the universe. I thought I deserved special treatment for my right behavior. I believed that I had earned exemption from heartbreak, primarily because I had spent so many years being such a good person.

What I didn't understand at the time, was that my system of beliefs was conditional. When life got hard, it began to fracture from the stress. I started to believe that the universe (and God) had let me down. He (God) wasn't holding up to his end of our deal.

Eventually I discerned that there were only two viable options—either my higher power was not who I thought (dependable, good, loving) or I just didn't matter to the universe.

Here is a bit of insight into my head during this time...

> *Dear Journal,*
> *I have this sense of fair and right. I believe that good behavior should be rewarded. If not an earthly reward, then definitely a spiritual or heavenly reward.*
> *I admit, I have always taken somewhat of a secret tally of*

behaviors, both my own and others. And to be honest, in comparison, I usually come out on top.
I have always had a deep-seated need for fairness and justice, and I desire justice from the powers that be. The universe should make the wrongdoing right, don't you think? I long for security and trustworthiness in my relationships and I believe I am entitled to them based on my efforts and behaviors.
I realize that sounds selfish and that I need to transfer my selfish desires into trusting in and depending on the universe to make things right...but why is this so hard?

Thankfully, there was a plan in place to strengthen my fragile, conditional, weak set of beliefs...

Strengthening our belief system can be likened to purifying gold. The process of purifying gold is tedious and difficult. It involves heating up and cooling down the metal several times which allows the impurities to surface so that they can be scraped off and discarded. With less impurities, the gold is now purer and stronger.

In a similar way, our set of beliefs can also be purified, and one of the most effective ways to strengthen those beliefs is through a life crisis. A crisis heats up our life and allows the imperfections and impurities in our beliefs to be exposed. Once exposed, we can work on removing them. In the end, as the gold is stronger and purer without impurities, so is our belief system.

I believe the universe has used my failures to grow, strengthen and purify my beliefs.

Is it a perfect science? Nope, not at all! I've no doubt there will be many more trials in my future. I know this because there are still many imperfections in my ability to trust my higher power.

Thankfully my beliefs are stronger than they used to be.

Belief is a big word. Even its definition is a broad one, so let's take some time and break it down into smaller, bite sized pieces.

Let's take a look at the three areas of our beliefs that are affected by our unforgiveness, resentment and bitterness.

The first is our:

Faith*: A high degree of trust or confidence in something or someone.*

I'm a believer that faith is something that we all have. For some, it may be a faith in humanity or the universe. For others it could be in a higher power, namely God or even Budda. And for some, it may be trusting in something as simple as a sign or coincidence.

While it is not my place or desire to define who or what you place your faith in, I do want you to understand that if you are holding onto disappointments, unforgiveness and/or resentments, then it is affecting what you put your faith in, whether or not you realize it.

I spent many, many hours and days crying out to my higher power in prayer. Oftentimes face down, pleading with Him to come and save me from my suffering.

God, help me...God, rescue me! God, YOU have to get me through this!

At times I felt abandoned by my higher power.

Consequences of bitterness Part 2

Where are you God? Why haven't you helped me? What is taking you so long?!

I was completely desperate.

I don't know what else to do! I'm praying and waiting and praying and waiting...and still nothing! I don't understand it. Why is the universe out to get me?

I was also completely **unaware** that it was my unforgiveness that was hindering the help I desperately needed and longed for. I wanted help more than anything, but I was unwilling to let go of my bitterness. I believe the universe couldn't hear my cries. My higher power wanted to help but it needed me to let go of the bitterness first.

In the recovery world there is a well-known saying–*Let Go and Let God.*

Whatever you choose to believe in, this saying speaks a universal truth. If we can let go of the hurts, disappointment, anger, and bitterness, the universe, or our higher power will help us. But we must be the first ones to let go.

It wasn't until I stood face to face with the reality of my only other option, that I was finally able to let go of my hurts and trust my higher power with my heart.

I was at a fork in the road of my life. Standing there trying to decide which path to take. On the left was the path of starting over. For me that meant divorce followed by a rebuilding of some semblance of a normal life for both myself and my children. The other option, on the right, was the path of trusting my higher power with my hurts and choosing to forgive my husband. This meant once again opening my heart to the person who had crushed it.

One path clearly made more sense than the other—starting over. I tried to tell myself that was the best path, the common-sense path. Yet I couldn't get rid of this nagging feeling. Something was impressing on my spirit, telling me to, "Try the trusting path. Take a leap of faith, you won't regret it. If you choose the other road, you will." I believe that voice was God.

I must say that I am (and always have been) a stubborn, strong willed woman. I held onto my right to be bitter like my life depended on it. I exhausted every other plausible option before I would even consider letting go of my hurts and forgiving. I see now that I have paid a high price for my stubborn willful defiance toward trusting a bigger and better plan.

I spent five long years stuck in resentment, fear, hopelessness, and bitterness. For five years I was completely unable to find any peace or joy. I didn't realize that my decision to remain in unforgiveness was robbing my life of all the good things.

I see now that those five years were spent in a self-made prison. I was in **total** bondage to bitterness, and I had no idea how to escape. In hindsight I know that my higher power was right there with me the entire time, constantly whispering to my spirit that there was a way out. All I had to do was let go of my hurts.

For much of those five years, I ignored that whisper and denied that any higher power was even there. I sat in my prison of bitterness, full of self-pity.

The second thing that can be impacted by our belief system is our:
Positivity = optimism and/or Joy

Optimism: *hopefulness and confidence about the future or the successful outcome of something.*

Joy: *the emotion evoked by well-being, success, or good fortune or by the prospect of possessing what one desires.*

For a season, I had lost any ability to experience anything positive. Everything in my life would be filtered through a sieve of negativity that left me feeling utterly discouraged and hopeless.

Often, I would just close my eyes and be quiet during worship time at church. Or I would try to pray rather than sing. It felt hypocritical to sing some of those words. Gladness and joy were not in my vocabulary.

I want to be clear that not all of us experience this blanket of negativity. I've met many people who've had very different experiences than mine in this particular area. For some, savoring moments of joy in the midst of crisis and/or heartache gave them hope. And while I recognize that and appreciate it and wish I could have experienced that for myself, for me, the moment my hurts turned into bitterness, it impacted my ability to be positive and find any joy.

The third area of our beliefs that can be affected by our bitterness is:

Our ability to be inspired.

I don't have to tell you that there are unlimited ways to find inspiration in life. Some seek education such as reading, taking classes or counseling. Others may find it more organically, through nature, listening to music or meditating.

I have found that the process of being mentally stimulated is in fact a prerequisite to acquiring wisdom in our lives. In other words, inspiration is essential to insight.

Have you ever heard of cognitive behavior therapy or CBT? It is a form of psychological treatment that has been demonstrated to be effective for a range of problems including depression, anxiety, alcohol, drugs, marital problems, eating disorders and more. CBT usually involves efforts to change thinking patterns. (from American Psychological Association)

In layman's terms, CBT can be explained fairly simply...

Thoughts become feelings and feelings become actions

What we think becomes what we feel, and those feelings influence how we then act. This can also be looked at as a three step process:

Step one: Our thoughts. This is the area where inspiration first happens—in our minds. Our minds are the most influential part of our bodies. What happens in our minds will, without exception, influence how we behave.

Step two: Our feelings. Our thoughts will first have a direct effect on our feelings. It's why we turn to unhealthy things when we are hurting—because it makes us *feel* better. 'Drinking too much makes me feel numb', or, 'food is my every happiness'. The motivation behind all we do—good and bad—are our feelings.

Step three: Our actions. As I just said in the last step...feelings always have a direct impact on our actions. We do unhealthy things because it feels good, or we stop doing unhealthy things because it feels bad. And visa-versa—we do healthy things because it feels good.

CBT has been a powerful tool in my life for so many reasons. It has helped me to understand the process of getting to an action, both healthy and unhealthy. Once I understood that in order to stop or start a behavior, I first needed to work my way back to the thought, and in order to get to that thought I needed to figure out the feeling that influenced the thought.

It can be looked at as sort of a simple math equation...

Thoughts = feelings
Feelings = actions
Thoughts + Feelings = Actions

It's simple but powerful.

Our thought life is where inspiration and optimism both start and when we hold onto unforgiveness for too long and become bitter, we can lose the ability to experience inspiration.

Now I want to make sure that you understand that at the same time I was lost in bitterness, I was also *diligently* seeking inspiration primarily through reading and meditation. I attended church and Bible study faithfully the entire time I was in my prison of unforgiveness. I completed *nine* in depth studies. I prayed more, read more books, and scoured God's word more during that period of darkness than ever before.

By all accounts, I had the appearance of being immersed in inspiration. I was hungry for as much knowledge as I could get, yet I never felt that craving satiated.

I believe the reason my hunger was never satisfied was because my bitterness hindered all three areas of my belief system.

Hinder: *to cause interruption, to obstruct. To interfere with the movement, progress, or development of something or somebody.*

My unwillingness to let go of my hurts hindered my ability to receive any inspiration.

I had an obstruction that kept me from being able to digest any inspirational sustenance. Almost like I was binging and purging any knowledge and wisdom I could find. I tried to fill up on inspiration through reading, meditation but then inducing vomiting. *I ended up malnourished***.**

It took time to realize that what was hindering my nourishment was my own unwillingness to let go of the hurt. My bitterness was caused by malnourishment.

Now think about this, what happens when our faith, positivity and our ability to be inspired are impaired for a long period of time?

Our Belief System Can Short Circuit

Short circuit: *to cause a sudden break in, to impede or thwart.*

When our belief system short circuits, it causes a break in our connection with the universe, and it hinders help from our higher power. What happens then?...

WE BECOME DISCOURAGED AND HOPELESS

Discouraged: *Having lost confidence or enthusiasm; disheartened.*

Hopeless: *Having no expectation of good or success.*

Consequences of bitterness Part 2

Discouragement and hopelessness have both been direct results of my long term unforgiveness.

In a previous chapter I spoke of feeling like I was in quicksand. The more I fought and struggled, the more I got stuck—that is discouragement. Then when you finally give up—that is hopelessness.

It's cause and effect. Our long term unforgiveness causes us to feel discouraged and our discouragement causes us to feel hopeless, which then has the added benefit of making us feel angrier, causing us to become more bitter. At some point we start to feel as though we are running a rat race.

Rat race: *A term used for an endless, self-defeating or pointless pursuit.* We go around and around, spinning yet never getting anywhere.

Allow me to explain the cycle of bitterness in greater detail.

Betrayal (of any sort) can become bitterness. Once it does, that bitterness then hinders the ability to be inspired. Then, over time that hindered inspiration takes its toll and can begin to short circuit our belief system, which causes us to feel discouragement. Discouragement over time leads to hopelessness, making us more bitter. Which hinders our ability to receive inspiration (or wisdom), which short circuits our faith, causing more discouragement and hopelessness, which makes us more bitter. And we cycle around and around, descending deeper into that pit of bitterness.

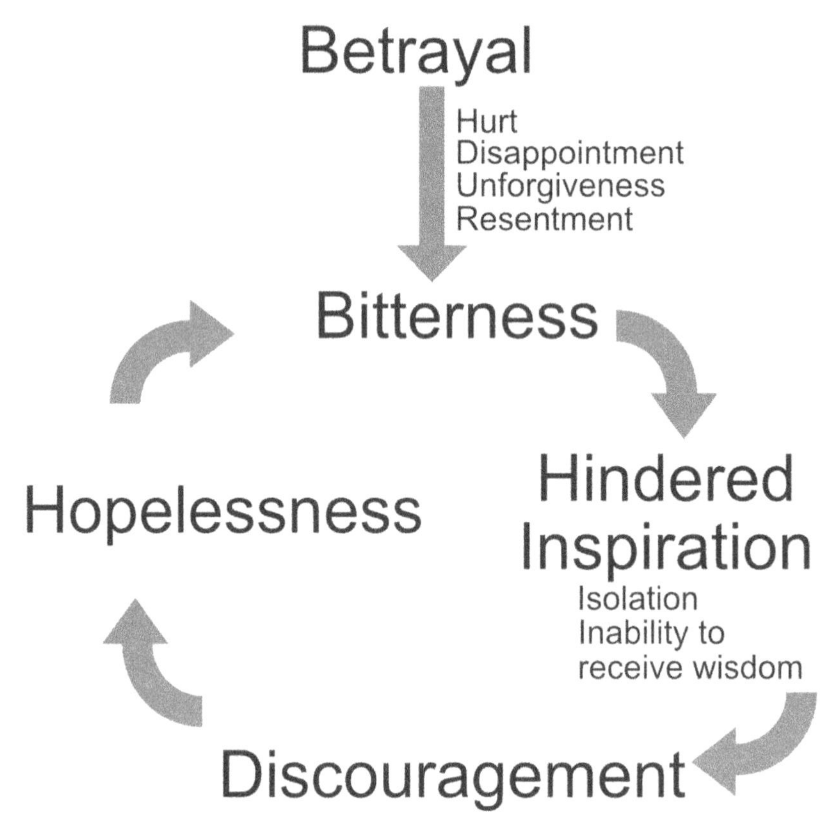

This rat race becomes an endless, self-defeating, pointless pursuit. When this cycle is drawn on paper it appears that we are indeed pursuing something. Believe it or not, it looks as though we are pursuing bitterness! Who in their right mind would do such a thing?

Nobody starts down the road of refusing to forgive with a drive to end up angry, bitter and miserable. When you started down that road, you weren't exactly sure where it was taking you, but then at some point you realized that the destination was not a good one.

The reality is, if you are currently on that road of unforgiveness and you choose to do nothing about it, you'll still end up stuck in the mire that is bitterness. It's a natural progression. You must do something drastic to get off the bitterness wheel.

Nothing changes if nothing changes!

If you're feeling stuck in a rat race or lost in the spin cycle of bitterness and unable to find your way out, there is hope!

HELP IS ON THE WAY!

Chapter 9
Stopping the spin cycle

As a child I loved to spin in circles just for the fun of it. I'd amuse myself with feeling disoriented as I joyfully wobbled around after a good twirl. Now as an adult, just the thought of spinning in circles makes me queasy.

I spent several years spinning on that wheel of bitterness. Like a little rat on a wheel in his cage. Trying to get somewhere yet going nowhere. I wanted to make the spinning stop, I just didn't know how to. I hated it yet I became an expert at it. I could teach a spinning class if it meant jumping onto a

life-sized rodent wheel to scamper about for an hour. Unless you have a brain the size of a peanut, the rodent wheel scamper (sounds like a new dance craze) quickly leads to discouragement and hopelessness.

King David from the Bible was familiar with feeling discouraged and hopeless. I imagine many days he felt like he was just spinning his wheels. David used words to describe his disheartened feelings like distressed, worn out, afflicted, helpless, forgotten, oppressed, abandoned, overwhelmed, just to name a few. Sounds like David knew the moves to the 'rodent wheel scamper'.

If you are stuck on that wheel of bitterness, then whether or not you realize it, you are in a hostile environment. If unforgiveness is overpowering you and you've tried to fight against it but in the end it's too strong a foe for you, then it is time to cry out to the universe to help you.

Bitterness is an ocean of hate, and it will become the void in which you will drown. It will attack you when you are at your weakest. This is not a 'play by the rules' kind of enemy we are up against. Bitterness has one goal, to destroy you, and it doesn't play fair.

But rest assured, your higher power is not telling you they will help AS SOON AS you get a better attitude. The universe is not twiddling its thumbs waiting for us to get a more positive outlook on life. There is help for us right where we are, right now—today!

All we have to do is lay our burdens down and let go of our hurts so we can reach up, trust and then receive help. Our higher power *will* take hold of you and help you off that spinning wheel. All you have to do is decide you need help...then trust. That's it. Easy, right?

The decision part *is* easy, especially when we realize we aren't getting anywhere on our own. I got great at deciding I needed help. I begged, pleaded and bartered, for my higher power to help me. The part that wasn't so easy for me was the trusting part.

What I really wanted was an easy way out of my painful dilemma. I didn't want to lay down my hurts and give them to my higher power or the universe. I certainly wasn't going to let go of my hurts willingly.

What I really wanted was a supernatural lobotomy.

Lobotomy: *A surgical operation on a part of the brain to treat pain or an emotional disorder*

I know this may sound kooky but there was a time where I wished for someone or something to supernaturally take away my knowledge of the things that caused my brokenheartedness. I believed the universe was capable of removing my awareness of the truth. And if that could happen then I wouldn't have to experience the painful, emotional effects of knowing the truth. Problem solved.

For a long time I thought ignorance sounded so blissful, especially in comparison to the agony I was experiencing due to painful awareness.

In my journey of figuring out forgiveness, I've discovered two things necessary to stop the bitterness cycle. That's it. Just *two* steps to letting go of the hurt. Sounds easy right? Truthfully these two things have been some of the hardest I've ever had to learn and then do. In this chapter and the next, we'll camp on these two steps.

The first step to freedom from our bitterness is:

Learning how to *really* trust your higher power or the universe

You may be thinking, "I already do trust, so I'm already a step ahead."

I thought that too. I gave myself more credit for trusting my higher power than I should have. Yet when crisis hit, my ability to trust flew out the window right along with peace and joy. I thought I had a good amount of trust in my higher power, until that trust was tested.

Test: *A difficult situation; an often-difficult situation or event that will provide information about somebody or something.* (Encarta dictionary)

I believe the universe uses hardship in our lives to test our trust.

> *"All life demands struggle. Those who have everything given to them become lazy, selfish, and insensitive to the real values of life. The very striving and hard work that we so constantly try to avoid is the major building block in the person we are today."*—Pope Paul VI

Many of us will experience times when the suffering is so intense that we question whether we're going to survive. There is a goal here. A purpose to the pain—to strengthen our trust in the universe and to see the bigger picture in our pain.

> *"It is when a crisis arises that we instantly reveal upon whom we rely."*—Oswald Chambers

My life crisis revealed who I relied on. I believe my higher power already knew what my weaknesses were, but those weaknesses needed to be revealed to me.

I relied on myself. I thought my actions were enough to create a safe environment where I wouldn't get hurt again. I thought I had done everything right.

Have you ever thought this about someone else?

If they could just see in themselves what everyone else sees in them. Then they could work on that thing and maybe change who they are for the better.

If you've thought that about others, chances are others have had that same thought about you...and me...and all of us. Why? Because we all have blind spots.

This process of revealing our weaknesses to us is essential to our emotional, spiritual and relational growth.

Why, you ask? Well first, it humbles us.

Humble: *Unassuming in attitude, respectful towards others, without pretensions.*

This step of being humble is imperative to our growth! We all must get to a place where we are unassuming in our attitude and without pretension. That is the only way we can receive new information and be open to a different way of thinking.

None of us are perfect and all of us have things to learn. I personally believe that when I'm done learning all there is to learn, the universe will no longer need me here on earth and I will transition to a higher place. In my belief system, that place is heaven.

I absolutely love that definition of humble. It is my deepest desire and daily hope to remain in a position of humility. To be unassuming in attitude, respectful towards others and without pretensions. Imagine the healing that could happen in our world if we all sought daily to be this definition of humble. Not to mention the personal freedom we would experience. To be free from assumption, or pretention. To just be and allow others to also be. Regardless of race, religion or political affiliation.

I could write a whole book on that definition of humble! But for now, let's move on... Being humbled is so important for one primary reason...it allows us to become teachable.

Teachable: *capable of being instructed. Able and willing to learn.*

Many of you picked up this book and began reading it because of a particular event that occurred in your life. Maybe it was a hurt, betrayal, or loss that you have not been unable to let go of or maybe it's a childhood hurt from decades ago that you just can't seem to get past.

Then at some point, you became aware that you needed help to get past this hurt. For some of you, it may have been a humbling experience to realize you can't figure this out on your own. Trust me, I get it and I've been there.

Helping those who have had their hearts broken was not part of my original plan. I wanted to help people have a happy marriage and I thought my first book would be on the topic of how to do just that. I even had all the chapters outlined. Little did I know the universe had different plans for me.

It turned out that I wasn't at all qualified to teach or write on the topic of a happy marriage. Quite the contrary, in fact. Instead, the universe revealed my weaknesses to me, and I was humbled. That humbling made me teachable and showed me how to truly let go of the hurts and forgive. And now I am beyond honored and grateful to be able to help others learn what took me so long to learn. Today, I wouldn't go back and change it, even if I could. This is what I was made to do, and this is what fulfills me.

The powers that be test us because that testing has a way of revealing our true character *to us*. When we see our own flaws and imperfections, it humbles us. That unassuming attitude and lack of pretension makes us more teachable, and that teachability is necessary in order for us to learn and ultimately change.

While we can't hide our true self from the universe or our higher power, we can deceive *ourselves* into believing we are something that we are not. In other words, we *can* fool ourselves into believing a lie about ourselves.

I was convinced that I was *firmly* rooted in my ability to trust in my higher power. I thought my belief system was unshakable—earthquake proof.

Do you know the only way to find out if something is really earthquake proof? You've got to see how it holds up in an earthquake. My seismic life event measured about a 6.2 on the Richter scale. I came to find out, there were all sorts of weaknesses in my so-called 'unshakable' trust. I had a front row seat to my life as it started to crumble to pieces all around me.

> *"All men make mistakes, but a good man yields when he knows his course is wrong, and repairs the evil. The only crime is pride."*—Sophocles (The Theban Plays. #3)

I spent years ignoring that still small voice whispering 'trust the universe. There's something bigger at play here so trust in the process'. I rejected all correction because for one thing I didn't do anything wrong that needed *a level* ***of*** correction. For another thing, I had every right to be hurt, unforgiving and resentful because I was the one who had been betrayed. I refused to trust in the bigger picture.

trust: *confidence in and reliance on good qualities, especially fair-*

ness, truth and honor. Trust involves two very important ingredients, **confidence and reliance**.

I had lost all confidence in good qualities such as fairness, truth and honor. Over time, my life earthquake destroyed everything I valued. It took me a long time to get back to the place where I could trust in the bigger picture and allow my higher power to handle my life rather than only trusting in myself.

Has the universe revealed 'stress fractures' in your trust or faith? Could it be that your weaknesses are being revealed in order to humble you so that you can be more teachable? The universe's ultimate objective is to strengthen you and gift you with more wisdom. Trust the painful process, knowing that you will grow in confidence and reliance as you learn valuable life lessons.

> *"Trust is like blood pressure. It's silent, vital to good health, and if abused it can be deadly."*—Frank Sonnenburg

> *"When mistrust comes in, love goes out."*—Irish proverb

> *"Trust is the glue of life. It is the most essential ingredient in effective communication. It's the foundational principle that holds all relationships."*—Stephen Covey

Trust is something we can choose to have, in spite of our circumstances. Can one be a good person and not trust? Yes, absolutely. I'm living proof. Thankfully the universe is constantly encouraging us to trust in something bigger than ourselves, whether that be a higher power, common humanity or simply our own ability to grow and learn from hardship. There is something in our subconscious urging us to trust in the universe as a well-ordered whole.

Let's take a look at a few of the benefits we receive when we trust.

1 Trust helps us be more calm.

Calm: *not showing or feeling nervousness, anger, or other strong emotions.*

Many have experienced a supernatural calmness *in spite of* their circumstances. It's easy when your circumstances are tranquil and serene. But how do we experience calmness or peace in the midst of chaos? We learn to trust. Trust that there's a bigger picture we may not see. Trust that on the other side of our crisis, we will have more wisdom and understanding.

2 Trust nurtures our psychological well-being.

Similar to point number one, our psychological well-being is more about our state of mind. To have our cognition nurtured (strengthened, stimulated) is a beautiful thing and one of the ways to boost our ability to process mental understanding through thought is to strengthen our ability to trust.

3 Trust decreases our desire to blame others.

Can you see the building block here? Trusting in a higher power or the universe or the bigger picture, lessens our need to find fault or seek justice when a wrong has been done to us.

Now of course this is not an all-inclusive statement. Wrong is wrong and always will be wrong. I have always been a justice seeker and one of my life mantras is 'right is right even if nobody is doing it and wrong is wrong even if everyone is doing it'.

I spent years expending all my energy blaming others for the wrongs that had been done to me. Yet there was nothing I could do to go back in time and change those wrongs. When I stopped pointing fingers and assigning blame, I became more willing (and able) to seek wisdom, knowledge and understanding. Less blaming allowed me to focus more on the lesson that the universe wanted to teach me.

4 Trust allows us to experience more gratitude.

I believe one of the lessons the universe wanted to teach me was to be more grateful. There were many things I took for granted, rather than saw as a gift. My young 19-year-old mind assumed that when I said 'I do', I would simply and naturally have a 'happily ever after' marriage. Little did I know that a happy marriage required effort. Today I can say that I am grateful for my husband, and I chose him for better or worse, richer or poorer, in sickness and health.

Trusting in my higher power has taught me to cherish the things I used to value too lightly. Physical health, a happy heart, a healthy marriage, a strong relationship with my adult children, the ability to play with my grandchildren. The list can go on and on.

The first step in getting off the rodent wheel cycle is learning how to really *trust* in the bigger picture or higher power.

"Okay but how?"

Well, you could try everything else and when all else fails, try trusting as a last resort. That's what I did. I don't recommend it.

Or you could work backwards and use what you have learned about **trust** to **trust**.

In other words, you can revisit those four benefits of trust *and* use those to fuel your resolve to trust. Maybe try it for a few months and journal what you experience.

You *can* choose to trust in spite of your circumstances! There is no magic trust potion here. No special ointment or prayer that will turn fear into trust like magical fairy dust. This is a methodical process.

Learning to trust is a systematic, painstaking series of actions with a specific goal.

It's taking baby steps, moment by moment choosing to trust your higher power with your hurts and fears.

I have a friend who walks around her block when she is anxious and with each step she repeats the words, "let go (left foot) and let God" (right foot). Over and over again. This simple activity has many benefits:

1. It teaches her to trust more every day.
2. It gets her outside of her head, speaking the truth so that she no longer focuses on her fears.
3. It gives her body exercise and, well, we all know the benefits of that.

It's plastering inspirational words/sayings/verses about trust all over: your house, your car, your computer, wherever you need reminders.

> *"You must trust and believe in people, or life becomes impossible."*—Anton Chekhov

> *"Wise men put their trust in ideas and not in circumstances."*—Ralph Waldo Emerson

It's constantly telling yourself that you are not going to do what you've done in the past, because it hasn't gotten you anywhere. Instead, you're going to take off that record in your head and put on a new record telling yourself that you are choosing to trust.

It's continually reminding yourself, throughout the day that untrusting thoughts do not help you and in fact may hurt you.

It's moment by moment, day by day, reliance and confidence in something bigger than your circumstances.

It's accepting that the universe is better equipped to deal with your hurts than you are.

Trusting is not easy, but it is worth it!

Learning to trust *will* involve **reliance**, **resolve** and **sacrifice**!

You must first make the decision to rely on something or someone outside of you.

Reliance: *dependance on or trust in someone or something.*

You must resolve to trust the process—the bigger picture.

You must sacrifice...

Sacrificing is usually the hardest of these steps.

Sacrifice: *a giving up of something valuable or important for somebody or something else considered to be of more value or importance.*

To trust again we must sacrifice our right to hold onto our hurts. We may even have to sacrifice our right to be right. Even if we feel we have every reason to be hurt.

Years ago my husband, Jim, needed to deal with an issue that arose in a recovery group he was leading. A few of the volunteers were upset about some of the tasks they were being asked to do.

Jim met individually with each party involved, asking them to share their concerns so that he could get a better understanding of the situation at hand. The first gal Jim met with, came to the table with a laundry list of complaints and concerns, mostly regarding how many of the volunteers were 'doing things wrong' and she insisted that they be told exactly what they needed to do to change. Jim let her speak until she had aired all her concerns and then he very gently spoke these words to her with an empathetic voice, "It sounds like you are used to being in charge."

For some reason, those words were exactly what this individual needed to hear. Her demeanor instantly changed from being harsh to humble, and the conversation also shifted from a rant to a sharing of hearts.

I believe this story makes an important point. While this person was on her indignant rant, the only thing Jim could see in them was pride and arrogance. It was almost impossible to look past their insistence of rightness and see that underneath the harshness they were hurting.

Then immediately when she dropped her weapons of attack and shared her struggle with needing to be in control, Jim immediately felt deep compassion for her. He was compelled to care for her heart and his attitude shifted from 'I *really* don't care for you', to 'how can I care for you?'

That story is a great example of how we can all be at times. Our indignant (angry or annoyed at the apparent unfairness or unreasonableness of something) behavior can be off putting to others, causing them to only see pride and arrogance.

Indignance hinders others from seeing the hurting person behind the harsh demeanor.

Synonyms of ***indignant***:

- Angry
- Up in arms
- Offended
- In a huff
- Resentful
- Incensed
- Put out
- Annoyed
- Piqued
- Cross

I was annoyed. Always annoyed. It didn't really matter why or what or who or when. I didn't need a reason to be annoyed, I just was.

Other than the word piqued (which I'd never heard before. It actually sounds like a happy word—especially when you see that it is pronounced [peek]), other than that word, every other word sounds so unpleasant.

Have you ever tried to care for somebody who is any of these things? Maybe your spouse or a family member is characterized by one of those negative behaviors. It's our nature to avoid, ignore or even despise those who are incessantly indignant, or angry. People like that can be such a drain on our energy and resources.

The moment we stop being indignant and embrace our broken spirit and broken heart, God will *immediately* draw close to us (we learned that in chapter 3) and notice us. He will immediately care for our broken heart.

By all appearances, sacrificing our right to stand up for ourselves seems weak, especially in a "me first" world. But sacrificing is actually a call to greatness and wholeness and health.

Trusting in a greater plan or our higher power <u>will</u> involve sacrifice.

When we choose to trust the universe or our higher power, we are giving up something valuable and important to us...*we are giving up control.*

Control:

1. *to exercise power or authority over something.*

2. *Ability or authority to manage or direct something.*

We give that control of our lives over to something bigger and greater than us when we recognize three things...[1] our higher power's ability, [2] our higher power's power and [3] our higher power's authority to manage our issues better than we can manage our issues.

The universe is asking you to place your broken heart, unforgiveness and/or indignance over to it. Your sacrifice will not be ignored when offered with a contrite spirit.

Are you willing to stop acting indignantly about your hurts? Are you ready to sacrifice your hurts and trust the universe to deal with them better than you have?

Stopping the spin cycle

"The universe is under no obligation to make sense to you." —Neil DeGrasse Tyson

"The universe's timing is perfect, even if it doesn't suit your ego."—Dean Jackson

"Thank you, spirit, for your guidance. We surrender this grievance to you, and we welcome you in to reorganize all limiting beliefs back to love."—Gabrielle Bernstein, *The Universe Has Your Back: Transform Fear to Faith*

Personally, I would never speak out loud the words, "I know better than my higher power about my life." My actions, however, spoke louder than my lack of words. I *acted* like I had a deeper understanding of what was best for my life. I behaved as though I knew myself better than my higher power knew me. This was not an intentional defiance, but rather a lack of trust in my higher power's ability to manage my hurts.

When it came to forgiveness, my heart was hardened and my understanding was darkened. I know that if I had continued in my hard hearted state, my circumstances would be very different right now. I'm so grateful that even though I let go of my hurts as a last resort, once I did, my higher power still helped me.

I hope it gives you hope to know that even if you are at the end of your rope, the universe won't say 'I told you so' as it watches you plunge to your destruction. Even if you wait until you've tried everything else before you decide to trust in something bigger than you, to help you, your higher power will still help you. It's *never* too late to trust in that higher power. Don't wait. The sooner the better.

Personally, surrendering my hurts and transferring my trust to my higher power has affected so many areas of my life. Obviously, it's helped to heal my marriage, but it also helped me worry less. Rather than worry, I trust in my higher power and the universe to manage those things I cannot manage—because I do not have control. Things my nature wants to worry about such as my health, relationships, ministry, will my marriage stay strong, my relationship with my adult children...the list goes on and on.

Once we finally acknowledge that there are powers greater than us in this world that can help us, and we come to the table with a heart that is broken and a spirit that is teachable, we will be given a peace that transcends all understanding.

The English word 'acknowledge' comes from the Hebrew root word 'yada' (pronounced yaw-dah) which means 'to know, to ascertain by seeing'.

Ascertain: *to find out or determine something with certainty*

You see, the only way to ascertain (find out, determine something) that there is something greater than us out there that can help us, is to acknowledge (know, see) that there is indeed a higher power and then to place our trust and control in that higher power's hands.

> *"To God belong wisdom and power; counsel and understanding are his."*—Job 12:13

> *"If you'll hold on to me for dear life,"* says GOD, *"I'll get you out of any trouble. I'll give you the best of care if you'll only get to know and trust me. Call me and I'll answer, be at your side in bad times; I'll rescue you, then throw you a party. I'll give you a long life, give you a long drink of salvation!"*—Psalm 91:14-16 (Message)

We need to seek the counsel of our higher power and trust that that higher power can direct and guide us.

Nighttime has always been when my higher power speaks to me with the most clarity. It's in the quietest time of my day when I'm the most willing to listen. Since I have never been a morning person (my favorite coffee cup expresses it perfectly: 'I haven't had my coffee yet. Don't make me kill you'. A bit extreme? Maybe, but it's a good example of how I usually feel when I wake up.

When we choose to trust, we are blessed and cared for by the universe. Choosing to trust is a systematic, painstaking process of deliberate reliance upon our higher power. It involves sacrificing our right to bitterness, anger and resentment. It requires laying down our broken heart, remorse and pain on a daily basis. Sometimes moment by moment. It involves letting go of our indignance and giving up control. *It will not be easy, but it will be worth it.*

We must be willing to give up our right to be right!

I've shared a lot of sayings or phrases in this study. When I was younger they sounded so cheesy, but when my life fell apart, I began to see power in those cheesy sayings. They helped to keep me on track when so much of my life was falling apart. Here's another saying I absolutely love and think of often:

I'd rather be well than right!

This one helps me. Every. Single. Day. Anytime I feel that old indignation well up, I'll repeat it several times in my head.

I can clearly recall the moment that my marriage counselor told me that I was now the cause of my marriage falling apart...no longer my husband. Even though he was the one who betrayed the marriage and wounded my heart. Her words branded my soul:

"You do realize it's now *your* bitterness that is ruining your marriage, don't you?" (her statement) "Actually. No, I don't see that. How is that possible? I haven't betrayed the marriage at all." (my response)

"While that may be true in a physical sense, you are now the one who is refusing to forgive and your unforgiveness has become deeply rooted bitterness. Your husband has repented of his sins and is now doing everything in his power to become a loving husband. You, however, have remained stuck in the sin of bitterness and it's ruining your marriage." (her statement)

Her counsel crushed me. I felt completely misunderstood and unfairly judged by her. Ours was a love/hate relationship. As much as I loved her wisdom, knowledge and discernment, I most certainly hated her that day!

Thankfully the universe used her words to humble me. I was that *indignant* person who refused to see that I was anything but the victim. I bawled my eyes out all the way home and cried out to God for the rest of that day. I was broken. Humbled. Finally teachable.

After five long years of crying out to my higher power for help, that was finally the day I was rescued from the pit of bitterness. In one swift motion, my higher power reassured me, comforted me and gave me great hope.

I would have asked 'what took you so long?' But I knew what the answer would be, 'what took *you* so long to surrender your hurts and trust in your higher power?'

I believe my counselor performed a much-needed intervention that day. Her counsel became a turning point for me. That was one of the worst days of my life, yet oddly enough, it was also one of the best. I tear up with gratitude every time I think about it. Only our higher power has the ability to take our worst day and somehow turn it into our best day.

I wish I could emphasize how much your higher power will do for you as soon as you lay down your hurts and trust in something greater. There will be no regrets. I promise!

May this be the day you are released from your unforgiveness.

Chapter 10
It's Time to Wave the White Flag

In the last chapter we learned that the first step toward figuring out forgiveness is learning what it means to really trust in our higher power. Now let's unpack the second step in our process of figuring out how to forgive.

Surrender

According to Wikipedia there are two types of surrender:

1. Military surrender. This is when soldiers stop fighting and become prisoners of war. A white flag is a common symbol of surrender.

2. Spiritual surrender. When one completely gives up his own will and subjects his thoughts, ideas and deeds to the will and teachings of a higher power.

Surrender: *the action of yielding one's person or giving up the possession of something especially into the power of another.*

Synonyms of **surrender**: *relinquish, give up, submit, forfeit.*

When I was finally ready to sit down and begin writing this book, it literally flowed out of me. In just 15 days the first draft was complete. I always knew that the universe wanted to use my process of figuring out forgiveness to help others, but I didn't know when, how or what that was going to look like.

The process of writing this book has been amazingly easy, supernaturally simple. That is, until I got to this chapter when we discuss surrender...this is where things got challenging. This is where the rubber meets the road.

How do I explain surrender in a way to make it desirable? Not to mention it's something I'm still working on myself. To be perfectly honest, surrendering feels painful, hard and somewhat unrealistic.

I relate to the military definition of surrender way more than the spiritual definition. I fought the fight of my life trying to hold onto my brokenheartedness and bitterness.

*"No retreat! **No surrender**!" was my battle cry.*

I was battle weary by the time I finally waved my white flag in surrender. After all, surrender meant defeat. Surrender meant that I had lost.

Trust me when I say, I was ready for a battle. I had all the battle gear on. However, I was losing the war for one simple reason—I was facing the wrong enemy. I thought my adversary was the person who had hurt me. It wasn't. Turns out, that couldn't be further from the truth.

You see, by design battle gear, also known as armor, is designed to protect our front—primarily our chest and groin areas. To be the most protected we can be, we need to be facing our opponent.

I got tricked into facing the wrong enemy, leaving my back side completely exposed. Boy-oh-boy did I ever get spanked.

> *"Be prepared. You're up against far more than you can handle on your own. Take all the help you can get, every weapon God has issued, so that when it's all over but the shouting you'll still be on your feet."*—Ephesians 6:18 (Message)

That verse goes on to say, "With this in mind, be alert..."

If you are struggling with unforgiveness, then you are in a battle my friend. And whether or not you realize it, you are *not* battling against the person who hurt you. Your true enemy is so much more menacing.

When it comes to unforgiveness, resentment and bitterness, we need to keep in mind that this battle is against the unseen, dark world - *not* against *flesh and blood*.

It's important to understand that there are dark forces in the universe that will try to convince us to believe that we ought not to forgive. We must be aware that there are schemes trying to get us to hold onto our hurts and not forgive. These spiritual forces of the dark world have a cunning plan to cause us harm. Don't buy their lies.

I say this from a place of experience as I believed those lies for a very long time. I fell for it hook, line and sinker. By the time I realized I was stuck in bitterness I was no longer warring against evil at all. I was warring against my higher power. I believed the lie that I had every right to stand up for justice and demand restitution for the wrongs that had been done to me. I thought my higher power owed me and I was determined to make things right.

The spiritual forces of the dark world are crafty and deceitful, cleverer than we could ever imagine. And their one intention is to mislead us.

I became their ideal subject. I bought their lies because they seemed reasonable. They made sense. They had the appearance of being rational, logical and practical. These dark forces are experts at tweaking an untruth just slightly, so that the lie now has the appearance of truth.

I had decided that if my higher power wouldn't punish the person who hurt me, then it was up to me to take matters in my own hands. Eventually I started to feel more and more angry with my higher power (God) because I didn't think He was doing His job. I thought he had dropped the ball, so I needed to take charge and make sure justice was served.

At one point, I had decided that the only person I could trust was myself.

If you are still at a place in your brokenheartedness where you are dependent on your higher power for strength, that is a wonderful place to be. But if you are holding onto your unforgiveness, and unwilling to let go of your hurts, then that dependence will begin to diminish over time and eventually you will begin to question their ability to 'set things straight'. Eventually there's a strong chance you will start to resent God. That is, unless you figure out how to let go and forgive.

That's what happened to me. My brokenhearted dependence on a higher power slowly devolved into questioning his timing and plan. Then it became questioning his ability to direct my path and finally it became disappointment and full-blown bitterness towards my higher power.

It took me a long time to realize that my unforgiveness and bitterness was only hurting me.

We've all heard the saying, 'resentment is like drinking poison and waiting for the other person to die'. Who would do something like that? Who would drink poison thinking it was going to hurt someone else? That sounds insane. And yet that's what we do when we hold onto bitterness. We're consuming toxins, expecting to see harmful results in someone else. It just doesn't make sense.

> *"Holding on to anger is like grasping a hot coal with the intent of throwing it at someone else; you are the one who gets burned."*—Buddha

> *"Don't leave the classroom of pain without gathering wisdom from its instruction."*—Tim Hiller, *Strive:Life is Short, Pursue What Matters*

> *"Whoever ignores instruction despises himself, but he who listens to reproof gains intelligence."*—Proverbs 15:32 (ESV)

That was the perspective I needed to hear. We need to pay attention when the universe corrects us or our errors in judgment. One definition of correction is to 'modify a behavior in order to make it acceptable'. (Encarta dictionary)

If you've stopped trusting your higher power to handle your issues, then it's time to 'heed correction' and modify your behavior. It's time to give up control of your life and surrender.

Many years ago I learned a powerful lesson on perspective. My 4-year-old daughter was in the hospital suffering from severe stomach pain. The doctors poked and prodded her tiny body for several days trying to figure out why she was in so much pain. In the end they were never able to find anything medically wrong with her. Watching her suffer, yet not being able to help her was excruciating for me.

One morning we decided to go check out the hospital's activity center to see if there was something we could do that would get her mind off the pain. We sat at a table and colored with several other children who were also sick. It wasn't hard to notice that some of these precious little angels were fighting for their lives. We sat next to a boy with hundreds of staples in his head from a recent surgery and others were clearly battling life threatening diseases.

Seeing what other children were dealing with in that hospital gave me much needed perspective.

I remember thinking, what we are going through is hard but...

"It could be worse."

Those four little words have gotten me through some tough days. Like when my husband lost his job. My first thought was, 'it could be worse. All that matters is that we stay together and stay healthy'. Jim losing his income gave me a new perspective regarding money and by the time he found a new job, we were well on our way to making drastic changes in how we both spent and gave our money. This trial in our lives gave us perspective. We took that perspective and used it to evaluate our behaviors as well as make adjustments in our priorities. It turned out to be a blessing in disguise.

Perspective: *a particular evaluation of a situation or facts, especially from one person's point of view.*

Synonyms of **perspective**: *viewpoint, outlook, perception*

Does perspective change our circumstances? No, it does not. But I believe we've been given the gift of perspective to help us cope with whatever difficult situation we are in. When we take a step back from our situation and look at it from a different point of view it can help us gain perspective so that we can move forward instead of wallowing in despair or bitterness. Perspective can give you a new outlook on your life. I encourage you to give perspective a try.

One very important point I need to make here is, saying or thinking 'it could be worse' is a helpful tool for us to speak to ourselves. Yet to say those four words to someone else can actually have an adverse effect, particularly when someone is in crisis. Speaking those words to another can make them feel as though you are minimizing what they are going through. When telling it to others, it should be used sparingly and with caution.

When we decide to look at our circumstances with a wider lens, it can change our perspective.

> *"Reject your sense of injury and the injury itself disappears."*—Marcus Aurelius

> *"Life is 10 percent what you make it and 90 percent how you take it."*—Irving Berlin

> *"To change ourselves effectively, we first had to change our perceptions."—Stephen R. Covey "Change the way you look at things and the things you look at change."*—Wayne W. Dyer

> *"It is a narrow mind which cannot look at a subject from various points of view."*—George Eliot, *Middlemarch*

These quotes helped give me a different viewpoint. Changing our perception will change our perspective.

When I became aware that focusing on my heart injury for too long was narrowing my point of view and that my perception had been dulled due to my own inability to let go of my hurts—I was motivated to change.

You see, the first step toward surrender is awareness. Once we become aware that our unforgiveness or bitterness is only harming us, we can then begin to take steps toward letting go of our hurts and healing our hearts.

The second step toward surrender is acceptance.

Accept*: to believe or come to recognize as valid or correct. To endure without protest or reaction.*

"Acceptance is the answer to ALL of my problems today. When I am disturbed, it is because I find some person, place, thing or situation—some fact of my life unacceptable to me, and I can find no serenity until I accept that person, place, thing, or situation as being exactly the way it is supposed to be at this moment. Nothing, absolutely nothing, happens in God's world by mistake...unless I accept my life completely on life's terms, I cannot be happy. I need to concentrate not so much on what needs to be changed in the world as on what needs to be changed in me and in my attitudes."

> *Shakespeare said, 'All the world's a stage, and all the men and women merely players.' He forgot to mention that I was the chief critic. I was always able to see the flaw in every person, every situation. And I was always glad to point it out, because I knew you wanted perfection, just as I did. A.A. and acceptance have taught me that there is a bit of good in the worst of us and a bit of bad in the best of us..."*
> —Alcoholics Anonymous

Once I became aware that my lack of acceptance was robbing me of any serenity in my life, I made the decision to work daily on accepting things as they are. That daily practice of accepting life on life's terms, was a huge game changer for me.

At first, learning to accept things as they are can be difficult. It certainly was for me. But I can tell you that over time, as I practiced acceptance daily, it became stronger (like a muscle) and today I can quickly get to that place of acceptance.

Awareness and then acceptance allowed me to relinquish control of my life, a life which I'd basically ruined by my own efforts, to something or someone who was more capable than I to manage it.

It's time to wave your white flag and surrender. Chances are, you've been fighting to keep your life from falling apart. Chances are that your efforts haven't gotten you very far.

Let's take another look at the definition of spiritual surrender on the first page of this chapter:

Spiritual surrender: *When one completely gives up his own will and subjects his thoughts, ideas and deeds to the will and teachings of a higher power.*

It's time to try something radical, something extreme! It's time to jump...

This is a leap of faith moment!

In 1995 I was given a vision. I know that sounds crazy, but in my defense let me assure you that I don't have these kinds of revelations or hallucinations often. In fact, this is the only one I've ever had.

I was in a prayer meeting with a group of ladies. We had split into groups and were praying for each other. There was a specific issue in my life that I needed God's guidance on. It was one of those issues that I felt could go either way. I could see that there was no clear right or wrong. Both options seemed to be fine choices, yet I had no idea which one to choose.

As I sat quietly, asking God for help, I received a vision. In it I saw God place me on the side of a cliff. When I looked over the side I could see down into the valley, but I couldn't see the floor of the canyon because there were clouds down below in the ravine. Looking down all I could see were the steep canyon walls followed by a blanket of white clouds. Then suddenly, from inside the fog, I heard a voice speak one word to me, '*Jump*'.

I believe that voice was my higher power encouraging me to take a *leap of faith* even though I couldn't see what I was jumping into or how far down I would fall. Something or someone assured me that I would be fine. Now this was not a verbal assurance, but I knew, and the voice kept telling me to jump.

It took me a few moments to muster up the courage but soon I envisioned myself taking that leap. I jumped. I saw myself free falling. I felt peaceful, calm and serene, almost like a bird soaring, yet at the same time I was completely aware that I was in fact descending into the mist below.

Suddenly, I saw a large hand come up through the blanket of clouds. I could see no other part of the body, just this giant hand that ever so gently caught me midair. I landed softly without a sound, and I knew at that moment I was resting in the palm of my higher power.

That's what trusting and letting go of our need to control our future looks like. We are in good hands.

Surrendering to something bigger than you is not easy, nor is it fun. In many ways it goes against our very nature. It is *daily* placing yourself under your higher power's umbrella of protection. It's reminding yourself that the universe is trustworthy and capable of managing your issues much better than you are. If I could say one thing that I know is true from my journey it would be that...

Surrendering is so worth it.

The payback is HUGE! What the universe has done for me in return for my surrender is so much more than I ever expected. I hope you will decide to trust your higher power and surrender to its will. There will be *no* regrets! I promise.

You may or may not be familiar with the serenity prayer. Growing up, it was always on a plaque, on a wall, somewhere in my house. I used to read it and think it was so cliché....so hypocritical. In my childhood home it was often quoted, yet rarely put into practice.

What I didn't realize until I was an adult (when I went through a recovery program) was that there is so much more to the serenity prayer. It really is a powerful prayer:

> *"God, grant me the serenity to accept the things I cannot change, the courage to change the things I can,*
> *and the wisdom to know the difference.*
> *Living one day at a time, enjoying one Moment at a time, accepting hardship as a pathway to peace, taking, as Jesus did, this sinful world as it is, not as I would have it,*
> *trusting that You will make all things right if I surrender to Your will,*
> *so that I may be reasonably happy in this life and supremely happy with You forever in the next." Amen*
> Reinhold Niebuhr

What a beautiful and powerful prayer. I could meditate on different parts of it every day and it would mean something new every time. Right now, the sentence "trusting that You will make all things right if I surrender to Your will" means the most to me.

> *"The greatness of a man's power is the measure of his surrender"*—William Booth

> *"The reason why many are still troubled, still seeking, still making little forward progress is because they haven't yet come to the end of themselves. We're still trying to give orders, and interfering with God's work within us. "*—A. W. Tozer

> *"Surrender is the ultimate sign of strength and the foundation for a spiritual life. Surrendering affirms that we are no longer willing to live in pain. It expresses a deep desire to transcend our struggles and transform our negative emotions. It commands a life beyond our egos, beyond that part of ourselves that is continually reminding us that we are separate, different and alone. Surrendering allows us to return to our true nature and move effortlessly through the cosmic dance called life. It's a powerful statement that proclaims the perfect order of the universe. When you surrender your will, you are saying, '"Even though things are not exactly how I'd like them to be, I will face my reality. I will look it directly in the eye and allow it to be here."*
> "—Debbie Ford

There is great power in surrender, not to mention freedom, growth and enlightenment. Take that leap of faith and trust that the universe will catch you. Let go, give up, and trust that there is a bigger plan for you. One where you are not only healed but healthy.

Chapter 11
Fitting the Pieces Together

Do you feel like you've been handed a 500 piece puzzle with no clue how to put it together? In front of you is a pile of blank puzzle pieces that are gray on both sides, and now the task at hand is to figure out how to put the pieces together. You may be wondering what side is up at this point.

I understand. Writing this study has put together many puzzle pieces for me. Hopefully I can help you put your puzzle together as well.

Let's use this chapter to review what we've covered so far:

Chapter 1:

We're only as sick as our secrets. That saying is so true and so powerful. Secrets make us sick. That's why I share some of my innermost secrets with you in this chapter. It's healing and so, so freeing.

It's my personal experience that I believe qualifies me to share on the topic of forgiveness. Not a college degree, or the number of my social media followers, or my birth line.

We discussed the purpose and problem of scar tissue when it builds up around our hearts, and how while it starts out protecting us, it can also do significant damage in our lives. It makes us guarded, unable to trust and more unhappy. If we don't deal with our unforgiveness, it will deal with us.

Then we explored the 3 paths of hurts. First, there's the path that chooses to cling to the hurt. That path leads to bitterness and misery. Path two is denial and while it may seem like an attractive choice to just pretend the hurt never happened, it's only a band-aid fix and like path one, it is detrimental to our health. We learned that denial hinders our emotions, keeps us from close relationships and can be a catalyst for other unhealthy behaviors.

Then we explored a 3rd path—this one is the most narrow path. It's the path that leads to healing, acceptance, peace and ultimately forgiveness. This is the path we want to be on.

Finally, we talked about how important it is to realize that you can't do this on your own. You need help.

The universe and your higher power can help you right where you are, no matter where you are. You just need to be willing to open your mind and your heart.

Chapter 2:

I shared my childhood story, starting with my first memory lying in a crib watching my uncle choke my mother. That experience taught me to 'hide-so-they-can't-hurt-me' and that became my way of coping when life got hard.

As the oldest girl in my family, I naturally became my drug addict father's caregiver, defender and cheerleader. I learned at a young age that significance came in the form of rescuing and fixing others.

I married my high school sweetheart at the age of 19 and I thought I was going to live a 'white picket fence' life. That is until he confessed to his first affair, four years into our marriage. Then over a decade later, my husband's lifelong sexual addiction could no longer be hidden.

While he began to work a recovery program, I was spiraling into a pit of unforgiveness. Bitterness became my addiction and was now the reason our marriage was failing.

Finally at the end of my rope, came a lifeline in the form of a supernatural intervention. I learned that I needed to give my hurts to a higher power who could handle them better than I.

Our higher power wants us to cry out to Him in our distress, we won't scare him off or upset him. We can be totally honest.

While secrets make us sick—the truth can set us free.

Chapter 3:

The theme of this chapter is, 'you are not alone'. So many can relate to your woundedness. Healing requires feeling connected to others who have had similar experiences.

Brokenheartedness is different for each of us. While one person may be heartbroken over something that seems small to us, we shouldn't compare our hurts to others' hurts. While the circumstances are often unique for each of us, the human experience of pain is quite similar.

We do a deep dive into understanding that our wounds need comfort first and foremost. Many of us have been given advice, opinions and judgments but those are not comfort. Knowing you are not alone is comforting.

Comfort: *to sooth, console, reassure.*

We discussed the importance of finding a safe place to share your story and experiences. I shared how, in my childhood, our family motto was 'any Ill will or unhappy emotions were to be promptly swept under a rug'.

Finally, I shared how my heart wounds made me question everything. I was plagued by 'what if' and 'if only' questions and scenarios. Yet when I realized I was not alone and that the universe and my higher power could help me, I started down the road of questioning less and trusting more.

Chapter 4

We discovered in this chapter that there are some real benefits to being brokenhearted. The universe will sustain you as you go through your pain. Suffering will grow us when we allow it to and when we seek comfort, we will be given the strength to endure the suffering, no matter how long it takes.

Following in someone's footsteps can help us navigate the pain of our heartache, and in turn help us to find some much needed comfort for our heart wounds. It's not a hard thing to do but it does require two important things from us:

1. Trust—we must trust that the person we are following can and will help us.
2. Focus—we must keep our focus on following in another's footsteps right now.

We explored how it's okay to be brokenhearted, in fact, it is a necessary part of healing. We learned that 'hardship is a pathway to peace'. And that after we've been wounded, broken hearted is just a little down that road on the pathway towards peace.

We discussed what it means to be 'spiritually bruised' and how sometimes even the process of caring for our wounds can be intensely painful. Yet the universe commends us when we endure suffering. Your suffering is part of a bigger plan.

Being brokenhearted sucks. There's no two ways around it, but once we accept that we can't change what was done to us, the best thing to do is find a healthy way to get through it.

You may need daily redirection for a while and that's okay. The universe or your higher power won't get tired of you asking for directions. He won't get frustrated if you get lost again and again. He is uniquely close to you in your brokenheartedness, and he wants to help you.

Chapter 5

By design, we all *need* comfort when we are wounded or hurt. We all *will* seek relief from our pain. Sometimes we do this in healthy ways and sometimes in unhealthy ways. In this chapter we discovered five sources of comfort:

1. Our higher power (comfort from a supernatural source)

Connecting to your higher power through prayer or meditation will help you to experience a peace that is greater than understanding...it's supernatural.

2. Shared humanity (comfort through connection)

Understanding that suffering is shared with all humanity allows us to connect to others and find hope and strength through our common experiences.

3. Wise counsel (comfort from insight)

We are blessed to have many avenues in which we can find wise counsel. From therapy to support groups to life mentors to self-help books and more. Finding wise counsel is the easy part, but receiving it requires authenticity, humility and being teachable.

4. Creation (comfort through diverse experiences)

Creation is a two sided coin. It includes nature and the comfort many find by being out in the elements and enjoying our earth. It also includes our individual expression of creative action. We all need a creative outlet in our lives.

5. Friends (comfort from emotional support)

There is nothing like that soul-level friend who can lift you up when you're down, bring you down when your head's stuck in the clouds and just sit with you when you're sad. We all need this sort of friend.

Four of these five sources of comfort come to us in ways that are higher or bigger than us. Meaning we can only find them through higher level thinking or inspiration. The comfort we get from friends is the only comfort that does not require an enlightened mind.

Supernatural comfort may not always be instant and immediate, but it is the only true and lasting kind of comfort. It's the kind of comfort that allows our wounds to heal properly.

Chapter 6

We learned that when we cling to our brokenheartedness for too long, that wound becomes infected with bitterness. Bitterness is an oozing sore that is off-putting to those around us.

Remember, brokenheartedness is not wrong, in fact it's favored by our higher power. He cares for the brokenhearted. But bitterness—that is a different story. Bitterness is wrong. We must choose to rehabilitate, or we will relapse. There is no middle place to hang out and just be wounded. Over time our heart wounds will either heal or they will become unforgiveness, resentments and bitterness. It's one or the other, as simple as that. Holding onto our hurts and clinging to our brokenheartedness for too long will cause some detrimental things to begin to manifest in our lives.

We looked at what it means to be bitter as well as ways to recognize if we have indeed become bitter.

Then we explored anger. Anger covers a wide variety of emotions. It's not just wild eyed, crazy, out of control rage, it's also being aggravated, exasperated, frustrated, impatient and cross. All are forms of anger. Anger as a human emotion is morally neutral, neither good nor bad. It's what we do with our anger that determines whether or not we are in the wrong. We give anger a foothold in our minds when we hold onto it for too long.

Our hearts will try to convince us to hold onto our hurts, rationalizing that clinging to them will in turn protect us from further hurt. While that may sound like a good idea, it isn't.

We ended this chapter on a positive note. Understanding that suffering can be a positive process of improving and strengthening us—if we allow it.

Chapter 7

Bitterness is a slow growing cancer, something negative that develops or spreads quickly and usually destructively.

We learned that there are some serious, often hard to see consequences to being bitter. Bitterness affects:

1. Our personality and character.

We can change from being positive Pooh to gloomy Eeyore. It can have devastating effects on our mental and moral qualities.

2. Our relationships.

Bitterness affected every relationship in a negative way. From friends to husband to kids to my relationship with myself—it trapped me in a pit of guilt and shame that I didn't know how to get out of. I knew my bitterness was hurting my relationships, yet I just didn't know how to stop

3. Our bodies—illnesses, weakness, depression, etc.

Stress takes a toll on our bodies. Being unforgiving, bitter and resentful causes a significant amount of stress and anxiety in our lives. Stress and anxiety are poison to our bodies. I can guarantee that if you are bitter, you've had your share of physical ailments and ignoring it won't make it go away.

If our emotional well-being affects our physical well-being, then it only stands to reason that emotional pain, when left unchecked and undealt with, will cause some significant physical issues.

Chapter 8

In this chapter we continued exploring the consequences of bitterness. Bitterness also affects:

4. Our belief system.

Our belief system includes our ability to trust in the universe, our higher power or anything outside of us.

Strengthening our belief system can be likened to purifying gold. It's a tedious and difficult task that involves heating up and cooling down the metal several times, allowing the impurities to surface so that they can be scraped off and discarded. With less impurities, the gold is now purer and stronger.

There are 3 primary areas where our belief system can be affected by bitterness:

1. Our faith (what we trust in)
2. Our positivity (our optimism/joy)
3. Our ability to be inspired (mental stimulation is a prerequisite to finding wisdom)

We discussed how thoughts become feelings and feelings become actions and we learned that bitterness can short circuit our belief system causing discouragement and hopelessness. It can become a cycle that we don't know how to stop. (Remember the rodent wheel scamper).

When we are unwilling to let go of our hurts, it hinders our ability to receive any inspiration. Don't let bitterness trip you up. Persevere, my friend!

Chapter 9

It's time you get off that rodent wheel. It's time to stop the rat race because it's not getting you anywhere. Asking for supernatural help is the first step but then you must begin to actively trust your higher power and the universe's plan to restore you to health.

We discussed the importance of having our weaknesses revealed to us and how it is essential to our emotional, spiritual and relational growth because first it humbles us and second, it makes us more teachable.

We learned that trust involves two primary things, **reliance and confidence**. Then we covered several benefits to trusting:

- Trust helps keep us calm.
- Trust nurtures our psychological well-being.
- Trust decreases our desire to blame others.
- Trust allows us to experience more gratitude.

Then we took a realistic look at what trust in action looks like—**a painstaking series of actions with a specific goal**.

> *"It is when a crisis arises that we instantly reveal upon whom we rely."*—Oswald Chambers

When we choose to trust the universe or our higher power, we are giving up something valuable and important to us...**we are giving up control**.

When we acknowledge that there are powers greater than us in this world that can help us, and we get to a place where we are truly teachable, we will begin to grow and learn, and we will experience a transcendent peace.

Finally, we talked about how Indignance hinders our ability to trust, and we decided to sacrifice our right to be right as well as our right to be bitter. We understand that **nothing changes if nothing changes,** and we are committed to change for our own wellness.

Chapter 10

This chapter covers the second step in letting go of our hurts—surrendering. Whether it be the 'battle weary' type of surrender or the 'spiritual' kind, or both. We all need to wave our white flag and lay down our weapons in submission to our higher power.

We discussed that letting go of unforgiveness is for our own good because bitterness only hurts us. Harboring resentment doesn't really hurt the person that we have the resentment against. We are only poisoning ourselves.

We talked about the power of perspective, and we learned that when we truly understand that our higher power is able to help us, that in turn encourages us to surrender. We explored the power in perspective and how when we decide to look at our circumstances with a wider lens, it can change our perspective for the better.

We discussed the two steps toward surrender—awareness and acceptance—and we learned that acceptance is the key to our serenity on any given day. Until we can accept things as they are, we can have no serenity. Awareness and then acceptance allow you to relinquish control of your life, to something or someone who is more capable than you are to manage it.

Surrendering is a leap of faith that is incredibly worth it!

What these 10 chapters come down to is this...

Forgiveness, while something we must choose to pursue, is also something that we cannot achieve on our own. It is a supernatural act. Only with the universe's help are we able to do this un-human-like, against our nature, thing. This miracle can happen in our lives, but we must trust our higher power with our hearts and be willing to let Him work things out in His time.

Now that we've looked back at what we've covered, it's time to look forward at what's next for us. At this point you have all the information you need to make one of the healthiest decisions of your entire life.

The next step is to recognize that...

It's now time to forgive.

Up until now, we have worked on creating a solid foundation upon which to build our forgiveness structure. We have done a lot of inward reflection by working on our own attitudes, and now it's time to put what we've learned into **action**.

Forgive is a verb. A verb is a word that in syntax generally conveys an action, an occurrence, or a state of being.

> *"Forgiveness is not an occasional act; it is a constant attitude."*—Martin Luther King

> *"You see that his faith and his actions were working together, and his faith was made complete by what he did."*
> —James 2:22

> *"We must develop and maintain the capacity to forgive. He who is devoid of the power to forgive is devoid of the power to love. There is some good in the worst of us and some evil in the best of us. When we discover this, we are less prone to hate our enemies."*—Martin Luther King, Jr.

Forgiveness: *to cease to blame or to cease to feel resentment against.*

Our faith must be accompanied by action and our actions will complete our faith. Don't let all this work be for nothing.

Saying you need to forgive is just talk. Words.

> *"If your actions don't live up to your words, you have nothing to say."*—DaShanne Stokes

It's time you take action. The payoff will be HUGE.

If you set your mind to be unwavering in purpose and you resolve to trust in the powers that be and you forgive, you will be rewarded. When we put our faith into action we will be blessed.

Believe it or not, once we have laid the groundwork for forgiveness, it's actually quite simple.

By Faith We Choose To Forgive.

The Bible speaks of a 'faith hall of fame' in Hebrews, chapter 11. This chapter speaks about many Biblical figures who took action by faith—in fact the words *by faith* are used 20 times in this single chapter.

I want you to close your eyes and imagine walking down that long hall, full of faith actions. Imagine each side of this hall with large paintings of the actions that were taken. As you walk along, imagine stopping to read all the famous stories about people who acted on their faith. On your left there's a portrait of Abel. He's standing in a field surrounded by his flock, and you read the inscription:

> *"By faith Abel offered God a better sacrifice than Cain did. By faith he was commended as a righteous man, when God spoke well of his offerings"*—Hebrews 11:4

Next up, on the right side, you stop at a painting of Enoch and beneath it you read:

> *Enoch, the son of Jared, the son of Mahalalel, lived 365 years. He was commended as one who pleased God. Because of his great faith, Enoch did not experience death. Because he walked with God he was taken away by God and was no more.* —Gen. 5:24-Heb. 11:5

Your mind begins to swoon as you are swept away by story after story of amazing faith. A little further down you see a very large painting of Noah standing in front of his ark. He has his hands crossed over his chest and his face is beaming with pride. You assume he must be thinking, 'Yeah...I built this!'

And just beneath that picture you read:

> *"It was by faith that Noah built a large boat to save his family from the flood. He obeyed God, who warned him about things that had never happened before. By his faith*

> *Noah condemned the rest of the world, and he received the righteousness that comes by faith."*—Hebrews 11:7 (NLT)

Next you read about Abraham who by faith offered his only son Isaac as a sacrifice.

On and on you admire the pictures and you read the stories of action after action that was taken by faith. You read about Jacob, Joseph and Moses.

Then you come to one of the few (2 in fact) females from Biblical times who made it into the Hebrews 11 faith hall of fame. It's Rahab and she is stunningly beautiful. Your eyes begin to well up with tears as you read her story:

> *"By faith the prostitute Rahab, because she welcomed the spies, was not killed with those who were disobedient"*—Hebrews 11:31

You are humbled to learn that our higher power can even honor a prostitute for her faith.

Towards the end of that long hall you begin to notice that there are a few empty spaces and you wonder, "Why are there still empty spots here? Is something missing?"

I believe our higher power is still adding new 'by faith' stories to that faith hall of fame every day. I believe...

There is room for you in the faith hall of fame.

Maybe it would say something like...

> *"By faith, they trusted a higher power with their hurts and sacrificed their broken heart so that they could figure out how to truly forgive."*

Chapter 12
Forgiving Yourself

Talk about a weighty topic. I mean, where do I even begin? I truly hope my perspective on this subject can help you navigate your journey through forgiving yourself. I have seen firsthand, both in my own life and in the lives of others, what a big issue this is and how it can trip many of us up in life because we struggle with forgiving ourselves. This was my husband's primary challenge for decades and it's taken a lot of work on his part to get to a place where he could finally forgive himself.

I believe the very first thing that needs to happen in order to understand what it means to forgive oneself is to:

1 Level the playing field.

We all must get to a place where we are willing to both give **and receive** forgiveness as we all have done things and will do things that need forgiveness.

I spent most of my young adult life thinking that others needed forgiveness more than I. I reasoned that since I've never done the really 'bad' stuff—never cheated, never stolen, never committed murder, it only stood to reason that I didn't need the kind of forgiveness that 'those' people needed. And since I'm not perfect, of course I'll need some lesser amount of forgiveness and grace for those days when I do those little wrongs and such. But thankfully I'll never need the big guns of forgiving myself, since I wasn't really a bad person.

What I didn't realize at that time was not only was I wrong in my thinking, but I was also wrong in my attitude. My, 'well, I'm not as bad as some' attitude was, in fact, judging. Judging was something I needed to forgive myself for...eventually.

As things turned out, I needed to forgive myself more than I had ever imagined, for my own critical spirit and holier-than-thou attitude. That was just the tip of the iceberg of the things I needed to forgive myself for. Over time, I learned that just because we may be unaware of something...doesn't mean it's not there. As the powers that be would have it, I would soon be made aware of my wrongdoing and the ways I was hurting others. I was guilty of things such as gossip, slander, hatred, jealousy, spite, judgment, criticizing, bitterness, grudge holding, self-righteousness and more. These things needed to be recognized, worked on, changed, and then forgiven.

You may feel you need forgiveness for things not mentioned above. Maybe you've done stuff that you are not proud of and in fact feel ashamed about. It's that shame that keeps us in a self-made prison until we drag those things into the light and deal with them so that we can let them go.

There can be a level of shame and secrecy attached to certain sins that can basically debilitate one's ability to ever truly heal.

The truth is, we can completely heal from our past wrong choices, and we can find peace through forgiving ourselves for ever making those wrong choices in the first place.

You see, no matter what you've done in your past, in the eyes of the universe, you are no better than anyone else and you are no worse than anyone else.

Leveling the playing field is a crucial first step because it helps us understand that forgiving oneself is a common humanity issue—meaning we all need to do this at some point in our lives because none of us are perfect.

Now, this next point I cannot emphasize enough. It is something that is essential to how we see ourselves and others. This one thing alone has the capacity to take your ability to forgive yourself and others to the next level.

2 You must make a choice to change your thinking —both of others and of yourself.

So much of forgiving others and forgiving yourself is about changing your thinking. Remember the cognitive behavioral therapy we discussed earlier? Thoughts become feelings and feelings become actions. We must resolve (determine, decide, make up our mind, settle on a plan) to change the way we think if we want to change the way we act.

It's changing those records in your head that tell you that you are not good enough. It's putting on a new record, with new self-talk.

That new record can be as simple as, *like everyone, I'm a mixture of good, bad and ugly. And like everyone, I am not all good, not all bad and not all ugly. Today I choose to focus on the good, while I work to change the bad and let go of the ugly.*

> *"What you stay focused on will grow."* - Roy T. Bennett

This saying is so true when it comes to forgiving yourself. If you focus on the wrong things you've done, and the guilt and shame you feel for doing those wrong things—your guilt and shame will grow.

> *"We live in a world where most people still subscribe to the belief that shame is a good tool for keeping people in line. Not only is this wrong, but it's dangerous. Shame is highly correlated with addiction, violence, aggression, depression, eating disorders, and bullying."*—Brene Brown

Shame fuels so many hurtful behaviors in our lives. It's time to change your thinking and stop the shame cycle.

> *"Don't dwell on what went wrong. Instead, focus on what to do next. Spend your energies on moving forward toward finding the answer."*—Denis Waitley

As someone who is self-critical by nature, I've had to train myself to change those negative thoughts. Some days I only have to change the record a few times, other days I do it dozens of times. Changing your thoughts is in many ways like strengthening a muscle—the more you exercise it, the stronger it gets.

All of us are somewhere on the scale of being either being too self-critical or too self-righteous. Self-righteous people tend to think too highly of themselves while judging others, while self-critical people tend to think too little of themselves and judge themselves.

I've been on both extremes of that spectrum, spending most of my twenties and thirties being self-righteous and judgmental, then when my life fell apart...and everything changed, that pendulum swung over to the opposite side, and I became too self-critical. Being too self-righteous, or too self-critical, are both damaging. As you can see, they both put **self**-first and they are both inward focused.

When we level the playing field and then begin to actively work on changing our thinking, then we can start the real hard work of:

3 Clearing your conscience.

Conscience: *an inner feeling or voice viewed as acting as a guide to the rightness or wrongness of one's behavior.*

Many of us are plagued with guilt. Guilt from past behavior, poor choices, wrong thinking that led us to wrongdoing. Guilt from angry outbursts, guilt from harmful actions and more...guilt, guilt, and more guilt.

Some of us even make up things to feel guilty about. I've been known to create reasons to feel guilty out of thin air. At times I've convinced myself that: I'm a bad mother, wife, friend, teacher, spiritual leader, housekeeper, cook, person...etc. etc. etc. And while there are moments of wrongdoing for sure (again, nobody is perfect), I certainly am not characterized by being bad.

Then to heap on top of how we feel about ourselves, there are also many things in our world that want to make us feel guilty. Our society says that we should be able to do it all. Then when we can't juggle family, career, household, health and more without feeling overwhelmed, well...we start to feel guilty.

New moms can feel guilty if they decide to work outside the home because they aren't home with their child—or guilty if they stay home because they aren't independent enough. No matter what they decide, they feel guilt.

It's the human condition to put pressure on ourselves to at least have the appearance of 'having it all together'. When I go to the grocery store with wet hair...I feel guilty.

There's a country song by Miranda Lambert that talks about this pressure women feel to 'appear to have it all together' even when they are falling apart:

Go and fix your make up. Girl, it's just a breakup.
Run and hide your crazy and start actin' like a lady!
'Cause I raised you better, gotta keep it together
Even when you fall apart.

Society and our mamas often tell us to 'hide our crazy'. In truth, 'hiding' is actually one of the worst things we can do. Why? Because...**Secrets make us sick!**

It's not easy to bring your secret stuff out into the open. I can personally attest to feeling humiliated, embarrassed and uncomfortable about exposing my junk to the light of day. But I can also tell you that it was worth it and I'm so glad I did it because when I did expose it, I also began to heal.

Clearing our conscience starts with:

a. Changing our thoughts. We've discussed this extensively already.

Next, if we haven't already, we must:

b. Face the truth and stop the wrong behavior.

Obviously if you want to be able to forgive yourself for wrongdoing, you must start with stopping the wrong behavior. We all know this, right? This step is definitely easier said than done.

Stopping the wrong behavior is imperative to forgiving ourselves. Each of us has experienced how it feels to fail at something we decided to work on and change. Here are some things that have helped me to stop wrong behaviors:

- Remind myself that I cannot be a different person until I act differently.

If I want to be a non-judgmental person, I've got to first stop judging. If I want to act differently, I must work my way back to the feelings that caused the action, and then the thoughts that caused the feeling that caused the action.

- Replace the wrong behavior with something better.

My husband speaks a simple phrase whenever he is faced with the temptation to do something wrong. He says to himself, "just do the next right thing." This quote reminds him to not only resist the temptation but then to also replace it with something better. This exercise is an incredibly painless, yet effective way to change bad or unhealthy behavior. Give it a try. I'm confident it will be a game-changer!

- Realize that changed behavior takes motivation plus time —plus repetition—plus focus…and then more time.

While we are working on clearing our conscience, we must also be diligent in giving ourselves an adequate amount of time to make permanent changes. Some scientific studies show that it can take as long as 254 days to form a new habit. Don't expect to change overnight, but give yourself time while you keep working hard AF.

> *"Ninety-nine percent of the failures come from people who have the habit of making excuses."*—George Washington Carver

> *"Repetition of the same thought or physical action develops into a habit which, repeated frequently enough, becomes an automatic reflex."*—Norman Vincent Peale

Keep reminding yourself that failure comes from the habit of making excuses and over time repetition will turn into a habit and that habit will over time, turn into automatic reflex.

The next thing we need to do to get to a place where we can forgive ourselves is:

4 Make amends or restitution when needed.

While this is a hard step to take, this one is so incredibly necessary for our own well-being. Learning to make amends is a life skill that, once learned, then embraced and practiced, will strengthen our relationships.

- Making amends is owning up to your yucky stuff and acknowledging your imperfections.

It's honoring to those we've harmed because it shows that we admit and accept the weight of our hurtful behavior. This step goes a long way in mending relationships and building trust.

- Making amends allows us to live at peace both with ourselves and with others.

When we strengthen this muscle of making amends, it has a restorative payoff in our relationships. Making amends will strengthen your relationships!

- Making amends keeps our ego in check.

An inflated ego can do so much damage to our forgiveness process. It can sabotage our ability to forgive others, receive forgiveness from others and forgive ourselves. Ego is not a bad thing, in fact quite the opposite. It includes our self-esteem, self-worth and self-confidence. But an unchecked ego can do a lot of harm. When we make amends, we are self-reflecting on our own shortcomings and that keeps us humble.

Ancient Romans had a tradition of celebrating their victories by parading their military leaders through town as they stood in their chariots. Part of this progression would include a servant standing next to the victorious commander who constantly whispered in the commander's ear the phrase, "memento mori" which is Latin for "remember that you will die."

Memento mori—or 'remember your death' is another way of

saying, "You are human. You are not perfect. You too are mortal." It's another way of keeping our ego in check.

It's so important for our healing to take this step of making amends whenever possible. When we face the truth and own up to our hurtful behaviors and then make an effort to make amends, that humbles us. That humbling is necessary for us to change and grow and heal.

That brings me to our next step in learning to forgive ourselves:

5 Embrace humility and practice it daily.

To be humble is to be unassuming in attitude, respectful toward others and without pretensions. To the healthy human, humility needs to be a way of life. Practicing humility is an ongoing process that requires a daily commitment to live your life with those three principles as guiding posts:

- Unassuming in attitude. Unassuming is defined as: not pretentious or arrogant.

Please understand that I am not speaking of one's personality when I speak of being unassuming. You can be unassuming in attitude and still be an extravert, or funny or timid or shy. This type of attitude is in no way connected to your personality—it simply speaks of being someone who is not full of themselves.

- Respectful towards others.

Some of the characteristics of someone who is humble: polite, thoughtful, mannerly, regardful, courteous. This is not conditional. It shouldn't matter if another person agrees with you or has your same political affiliation or belief system. Being respectful of others regardless of what they believe is a clear sign of humility and open-mindedness.

- Without pretension.

Pretentious: *attempting to impress by affecting greater importance, talent, culture, etc., than is actually possessed.*

This quote by Andrew Murray is a beautiful depiction of what humility looks like in action. Many people memorize this saying and recite it as a daily reminder or prayer of remembrance to remain humble in thought and action:

> *"Humility is perfect quietness of heart. It is to expect nothing, to wonder at nothing that is done to me, to feel nothing done against me. It is to be at rest when nobody praises me, and when I am blamed or despised. It is to have a blessed home in the Lord, where I can go in and shut the door, and kneel to my Father in secret, and am at peace as in a deep sea of calmness, when all around and above is trouble."*— Andrew Murray

Remember how we learned in an earlier chapter that humility is so necessary in order for us to change - because it makes us teachable? Teachability is a prerequisite to changed behavior.

Consider memorizing this humility quote or print it out and repeat it daily to help remind you of the importance of having a humble spirit.

The next step in learning to forgive ourselves is to:

6 Let go of the weight and release the past.

This is the final step toward forgiving yourself. Once you've evened the playing field, changed your thinking, done the hard work of clearing your conscience, made amends, embraced humility as a way of life—then you get this step of releasing the weight of your past and letting go of the hurt you have done.

Long term guilt that clings to us, even after we have made amends, will always affect our relationships in a negative way.

Letting go of the weight helps us to feel better about our good behavior and not beat ourselves up over our bad past behavior. This allows space to let a clear conscience come in. Take steps to release what remains after restitution.

Others may tell you that you don't deserve to be cleansed or forgiven of your past. I've said this to my husband. For years after he broke my heart, I told him that he didn't deserve to be forgiven. And I believed what I was saying. In my mind he didn't deserve to have his conscience cleared, because what he did was so wrong.

Eventually I would have to figure out how to forgive myself for being so hateful and bitter towards the love of my life. Sometimes I wonder why he stayed with me for so long. I was verbally abusive to him for years.

Don't let those old records continue to play that say you aren't worthy of forgiveness. YOU ARE! No matter what you tell yourself or what others may say. **Truth is truth is truth.** Truth will always be truth, even if you choose not to believe it.

You can have a clear conscience without being innocent. You can be guilty of wrongdoing and have a clear conscience.

If you struggle with your past and letting go of the things you've done, or the person you were, or the choices you made, or even if you feel guilty for something that you allowed to happen, or could have stopped from happening—if this is you then working through these 6 steps of forgiving yourself will be a benefit.

None of us are innocent. The Bible says in Romans 3:23 that, "all have sinned..." Translation, "none of us are innocent."

It's time to take off those wrong thinking records and put on the truth. Do it over and over again, as many times as it takes.

Now please understand that forgiving ourselves does not mean we won't suffer consequences for our bad or wrong behaviors. We probably will. Betrayed marriages can and do end in divorce—it's a natural consequence of betraying the marriage vows.

Just as poor eating will result in poor health, poor choices will likely result in painful consequences. Yet in spite of the consequences, we still must pursue forgiveness.

Eventually these steps will start to make a difference. Slowly, over time, you will start to recognize the wrong thinking and replace it with the right truth. I still have a lot of wrong thinking in my life, but I quickly recognize it and replace it with the right truth.

Today it no longer feels like I'm making a choice to forgive, it feels like I've made a change.

"The greatest discovery of all time is that a person can change his future by merely changing his attitude"—Oprah Winfrey.

"If you don't like something, change it. If you can't change it, change your attitude."—Maya Angelou

"The secret of change is to focus all of your energy not on fighting the old, but on building the new"—Socrates

Chapter 13
Your forgiveness toolbox

Even after I had forgiven there were still a lot of obstacles that kept trying to get in my way and throw me off the path of forgiveness that I was on. In this chapter I'll share the things that helped me stay on that path towards healing and peace. Many essential tools helped to keep me on course, especially on the hard days when my entire being longed to go back to the familiar prison of bitterness that I had become so accustomed to.

Some days, remaining in forgiveness was moment by moment. Other days I'd struggle once or twice throughout the day. Today, I can go months without feeling a struggle to remain in forgiveness. It certainly gets easier over time.

The tools I share in this chapter became a forgiveness compass as they kept me pointed in the right direction. I hope they help you do the same.

The first thing that helped me remain in forgiveness was to remind myself that:

1 Even after I have forgiven, I will NEVER forget.

"The stupid neither forgive nor forget; the naive forgive and forget; the wise forgive but do not forget."—Thomas Szasz

It is for good reason and by design that we will not forget the wounds we have suffered. When we go through hardship, suffering or loss, the goal is to come out of it with more understanding and wisdom.

It's important that we remember what it feels like to be imprisoned in our bitterness. It is healthy to be able to recall not only where we were, but also what we learned from where we were. We do not want to forget the work it took for us to be delivered from our unforgiveness, resentments and bitterness.

Believe it or not, the fact that we will never forget is actually a gift. The universe uses our struggles to teach us to have compassion for those who are hurting. If we allow it, our past pain can help us connect and encourage others who are going through painful things.

***It is by design* that we will not forget the wounds we have suffered.**

"Turn your wounds into wisdom."—Oprah Winfrey

"See, I have refined you, though not as silver; I have tested you in the furnace of affliction."—Isaiah 48:10

"Pain insists upon being attended to. God whispers to us in our pleasures, speaks in our consciences, but shouts in our

> *pains. It is his megaphone to rouse a deaf world."*—C.S. Lewis

My counselor would often say that even after I am completely healed from my brokenhearted injuries, I may always walk with what she called a 'life limp'. Some of us may have permanent reminders of past injuries. I remember clearly making the decision that if I am left with a life limp, I will embrace it as something that has been divinely assigned to me as a reminder of my injury and my rehabilitation.

If you walk with a life limp, acknowledge it, accept it and then learn to find the beauty in it.

> *"Behind every beautiful thing, there's some kind of pain."*– Bob Dylan

The second tool that can help you remain in daily forgiveness is understanding that:

2 It takes time for the pain to subside.

You *need* time to allow the painful memories of your heart injuries to diminish. Some say it can take up to half the amount of time you've invested into a relationship to get over the hurt, loss or betrayal of that relationship.

So, let's do the math. That means if you were married for 20 years, then experienced the loss of your spouse, it could realistically take you 10 years to *fully* recover from your brokenhearted injuries. It takes a lot of time and a lot of patience.

Another general belief is that the worst of the hurt lasts around five years. There still may be ache, but for the most part the pain does become more bearable. Even once you've let go of the hurt; you may experience a life limp in the form of sadness or loss. **Feeling sad is not a sign you have not healed from your hurt.**

I share these timelines, not to make you feel overwhelmed by the amount of time it takes to get over a loss, but rather to encourage you in knowing that it is okay for your heart to hurt for a long time. **Pain does not have a statute of limitations.**

Within a year's time, people started making comments to me that it was time to get past the pain and move on. Some would say that it was time to stop wallowing and that I just needed to suck it up and get on with my life.

Today I understand that it takes a lot of time for the pain to subside. Pain is often the last thing to go. Even after several years, when I think back to my heartbreak, it still can bring tears to my eyes. Just thinking about it can be painful at times. But here is the good news...

We can pursue forgiveness in the midst of our pain.

We all need time to heal. Sometimes it's a long, long time. We must make sure we are not becoming bitter, but then we must allow a margin in order to heal slowly. Heart wounds need to heal from the inside out. The amount of time it takes for you to heal will be different from the time it takes for others to heal. Take your healing one day at a time. Trust you'll get through today and don't worry about tomorrow until tomorrow.

Keep up the good work. You can do this! If you have a setback, just tell yourself that a setback is a setup for a comeback. Then get right back at it.

The third tool that helps maintain daily forgiveness is understanding that:

3 Forgiveness does NOT make it okay.

This is really simple but also very important. You may reason that if you forgive, that's like saying what was done to you was okay, and it's *not*. That sort of thinking kept me stuck in the muck for a very long time. What was done to me was not alright and it will never be, yet my mind kept playing the record that told me to forgive meant it was okay.

I want to reassure you that forgiveness doesn't make *it* alright, it makes *you* alright. Sometimes I have to tell myself that several times a day.

Forgiveness doesn't make the betrayal (or loss or hurt) okay, forgiveness makes *me* okay.

Forgiveness doesn't change the circumstance—forgiveness changes you!

Forgiveness won't necessarily heal the relationship—forgiveness will heal you!

Forgiveness won't fix the damage done—forgiveness will fix you!

Now let's talk about some tools that you can use right now, today, in your efforts towards pursuing forgiveness as well as remaining in forgiveness:

Tool # 1: Learning how to use your thought bubble.

Have you ever read the Sunday comics where there's a bubble over someone's head with a dot-dot-dot signifying that you are reading their thoughts? That's a thought bubble and learning to use your own thought bubble can be a game changer when it comes to helping you remain in forgiveness.

Believe it or not—**we don't need to say everything we are thinking.** It's actually not a healthy thing to do. When we learn how to keep our thoughts in our thought bubble, especially when our thoughts are **critical**, **negative**, or **accusatory**, we are taking an imperative step toward remaining in daily forgiveness.

Using your thought bubble is just a different way of saying, "if you can't say anything nice, don't say anything at all." Think of it as a zipper for your mouth and start zipping your lips before your hurtful words escape.

If you are harboring disappointment, unforgiveness, resentment or bitterness then you've probably gotten pretty good at speaking your mind. Most of what you think, you say. That's how I became, and my lack of a filter was doing damage to many of my primary relationships.

At first, I would write down my negative or critical thought and place it in a box I had made called an 'offense box', and I would tell myself to not react for a minimum of 24 hours. If after 24 hours passed I still felt the same way, I would then speak my mind. This exercise became pivotal in my healing as I can honestly say not once have I felt as offended, critical or negative after 24 hours. Not once.

Allowing a day to go by before I speak my mind, allowed me to think more rationally and when/if I did respond after that 24 hour period, it was always in a more calm level-headed manor.

This tool will also help you manage your emotions so that you aren't always blurting out what you are feeling right when you are feeling it.

> *"Words have energy and power with the ability to help, to heal, to hinder, to hurt, to harm, to humiliate, and to humble."*—Yehuda Berg

> *"The more talk, the less truth; the wise measure their words."*—Proverbs 10:19 (Message)

> *"The best time for you to hold your tongue is the time you feel you must say something or bust."*—Josh Billings

Christian faith teaches us to capture our thoughts as a way of life. **Capture:** *to take into one's possession or control by force.*

Synonyms of capture are: **catch, seize, take prisoner, detain, secure.**

That's what we're trying to do with our thoughts. Doesn't sound easy, especially if you've let your mind run wild with all kinds of negative thoughts and feelings.

I began working on strengthening my thought capturing abilities at night in bed. That was when my mind wandered the most toward pessimistic thoughts. At first, it felt like I was chasing a rabbit through a maze. As soon as I got close to capturing it, it would dart away. Those thoughts can be slippery little bastards.

Today I can quickly capture any unconstructive thoughts, feelings or judgments and make them behave—even if by force. Today I change the record and replace the thought. Over time it has gotten easier, much like a muscle when exercised gets stronger.

Start your thought capturing workout today!

Tool #2: Learn to give the benefit of the doubt.

This one may need a little clarification. It's a bit specific as it is for us to use when we have been hurt by someone who is still in our lives. Some of us have been hurt by people who should no longer be in our lives because they are not safe and cannot be trusted. This is not for them. We don't need to give them the benefit of the doubt.

This tool works well with those who inflict smaller wounds on a consistent basis. For example, in-laws who constantly harp on about your house cleaning abilities or tell you how to parent. This also helps with those who have hurt us but are actively trying to be better. They're doing a lot, but they are still far from perfect. For example, the husband who is going to counseling and working on his anger issues but still has the occasional outburst. This tool will help with that.

Giving the benefit of the doubt means that we ***choose*** *to believe something good about someone, rather than something bad, especially when there is the possibility of doing either.*

After my heart was broken, I *couldn't* give the person who had hurt me the benefit of the doubt anymore. Quite the opposite; they were guilty until proven innocent. Even the good things they did, my mind would look for the bad in it all.

If you struggle with giving the benefit of the doubt, you may have to re-learn how to evaluate intentions. Ask yourself, "Did they intend to hurt me, or did they aim to upset me?" Evaluating someone's actions based on what the objective was, rather than the outcome.

I became so overly sensitive toward the person who wounded me that they couldn't even pay me a compliment without me reading some ill will or evil intent into it.

Try to evaluate the intent of something when you feel hurt or wounded. Be realistic and when in doubt, choose to give the benefit of the doubt.

I still have days when my old 'what if' thoughts come flooding in, and my mind is inundated with negative, critical feelings. Within a few moments, I'm reminding myself that I choose to believe in something good rather than something bad. Is there the possibility that I may get hurt again? Of course. It would be naive to think there isn't. I am fully aware that we are all human and therefore imperfect. Do I have confidence that I will never be brokenhearted again? No, not at all.

Yet I know what it feels like to live everyday expecting the other shoe to drop or the sky to fall—just waiting for something bad to happen. So I can say firsthand that I feel better when I choose to give the benefit of the doubt.

These days, I no longer have the desire to police or control the thoughts or actions of others. I have found that trying to do so only drives ME crazy with insecurities and fears. Today, those kinds of feelings still pop up in my head from time to time, but I'm better than ever at capturing those thoughts and changing them.

If you're trying to forgive someone who is still in your life, then learning to give the benefit of the doubt is an essential, crucial step.

Keep in mind that these concepts need to be exercised with a lot of discernment and some very clear boundaries. Giving the benefit of the doubt is not about hiding the truth or sweeping things under a rug. It doesn't mean you should allow others to take advantage of you. Giving the benefit of the doubt works best when the person who has hurt you, has also confessed to the harm they have done and has acknowledged their wrongdoing and is working to make amends.

Tool # 3: When you're feeling overwhelmed...detach but don't withdraw.

This concept can be challenging to understand and even more difficult to put into practice. What it generally means is, when we feel ourselves becoming defensive or accusatory toward someone, or we start feeling negative emotions toward another (anger, fear, resentment, bitterness etc.), if we 'detach but don't withdraw' from them we can more easily regulate our emotions in the moment without harming the relationship. This is a way to keep the relationship from being tainted by our roller coaster of emotions.

In my opinion this is the *only* way to really care for someone who has offended you. Its benefits are twofold:

- **First,** detaching allows us to remain calm, or not get overly upset to the point that we may say or do something we will later regret. It gives us the space to respond rather than react to a stressful or upsetting situation.
- **Second**, when we detach but don't withdraw it allows us to remain close enough to care for that person who is doing or saying hurtful things. We can still work on the relationship, just without the negative emotions.

Detach: *to separate, disconnect or unfasten something.*

Withdraw: *to retreat from one's position, especially during battle.*

This concept has helped heal my marriage more than any others. It has also helped in other relationships (children, friends, in ministry, etc.). In times of stress or conflict my nature is to do one of two things. I either **attack and remain** (the opposite of detach and withdraw) or I **detach <u>and</u> withdraw**. Both are damaging to relationships.

Attack and remain is when you are so emotionally charged that you can't control your tongue. It's a 'in your face' assault. You're angry and that person is going to know that you're angry!

Detach and withdraw is when we pull away emotionally, relationally and physically. It's giving the silent treatment as a form of punishment. It's pulling away and shutting down, not addressing the issue but rather sweeping it under the rug.

This *detach but don't withdraw* strategy works well with emotional teenagers too. I've gotten good at detaching from my adult children when I feel triggered by their actions or words. This tool allows me to speak in a reasonable manner, while letting that person know that I am invested in them, but I am not available to be drawn into conflict with them.

When I began to practice detaching without withdrawing, I saw positive results almost immediately. I am confident you will too.

Tool #4: Realize that unrealistic expectations are future planned resentments.

We need to check our expectations and ask ourselves—are they realistic? Are they practical and reasonable? If not, we need to understand that (most likely) those unrealistic expectations will, at some point, become resentments. Remember what happens to unresolved resentments? They become bitterness.

The quickest way to catapult us right back to bitterness is to have unrealistic expectations. Either of ourselves or others. It usually starts with disappointment. Once we are disappointed we will soon begin to resent (dislike, be offended by, hate, begrudge, feel bitter toward) the person who let us down. It may be ourselves or it may be another person.

This one concept was a total game changer for me. **If you only work on one of these things in this chapter, please let it be learning how to change your expectations.**

I've found that changing my expectations has allowed me to celebrate everyday things in a way that I couldn't before. When I stopped expecting certain things, I wasn't constantly disappointed when that certain thing didn't happen.

Allow me to share a simple example. Suppose you expect your child to load the dishwasher after supper, yet they rarely do. It causes a lot of conflict in your relationship with your child because they are never meeting your expectations, so you find yourself constantly yelling, screaming and complaining. Or on the other side of that coin, you internalize it and find yourself disappointed and annoyed with them all the time.

Now, what would happen if you changed your expectation of this child and no longer expected them to load the dishwasher? Imagine how you would feel if you came home one day to find that they loaded the dishwasher, without even being asked or told or expected to do so. What a nice surprise, right? Now you get to celebrate their act of kindness, and you have eliminated any potential resentment by having the expectation.

Now I realize that this example has many flaws, and I am by no means suggesting that you allow your family to never participate in household chores. But I think it makes my point—so I'm going with it.

When you evaluate your expectations and change them, it allows you to appreciate more and resent less.

Just that little change (going from always resenting the person who hurt me to now being able to appreciate the simplest of things) did wonders to my overall attitude and general state of being. It helped me to go from always complaining to now being able to be content. Over time, I transformed from Miss grumpy-pants to Miss happy-pants, just by changing my expectations.

We need to change our **unrealistic** expectations into ones that can actually be achieved—**in real life**. Here are a few unrealistic expectations I have had:

- "I expect to never be brokenhearted again."
- "I want to look good in a bikini."
- "I want to stay caught up with housework."

We need to stop idealizing how we think our life should be and accept that **it is what it is**. This is rational thinking that is **focused on reality**.

When our lives are focused on reality, and we have the tools to manage all that life throws at us on any given day, we will find ourselves more able to:

1. Appreciate the good things—be grateful.
2. Manage the bad things—expect struggles.
3. Use our tools to handle the ugly things—overcome hurts.

I've spent the past decade learning how to figure out how to forgive and then live in the place of acceptance and peace. And I am so grateful for the journey it's been in order to get to the place I am today. And today I can say that I wouldn't go back and change the past even if I could. Once you know what forgiveness looks like and more importantly feels like, I believe you will say the same.

Here is my favorite quote about forgiveness. It's a reminder that forgiveness is a beautiful fragrance in my life.

"Forgiveness is the fragrance
That the violet sheds
On the heel that has crushed it."
— Mark Twain

May the forgiveness you offer to others and yourself, be a sweet, wholesome aroma that brings healing and life.
Kim

About the Author

Kim Corder, 58, is a writer, speaker, educator, and dedicated volunteer. Her life's journey, marked by childhood struggles and the complexities of a 40-year marriage, has equipped her with countless life lessons. Through these experiences she has learned the profound power of letting go and forgiveness, ultimately finding acceptance and peace. Now Kim teaches other women how to forgive, guiding them in their own paths to healing. Kim cherishes her roles as a mother to four adult children and a grandmother to 6 cherished grandchildren.

www.ingramcontent.com/pod-product-compliance
Lightning Source LLC
Chambersburg PA
CBHW031200270326
41931CB00006B/344

* 9 7 9 8 9 9 9 6 7 7 2 2 8 *